D09933299

Making Large Schools Work

The Advantages of Small Schools

Arthur Shapiro

ROWMAN & LITTLEFIELD EDUCATION
A division of
ROWMAN & LITTLEFIELD PUBLISHERS, INC.
Lanham • *New York* • *Toronto* • *Plymouth, UK*

Published by Rowman & Littlefield Education
A division of Rowman & Littlefield Publishers, Inc.
A wholly owned subsidiary of The Rowman & Littlefield Publishing Group, Inc.
4501 Forbes Boulevard, Suite 200, Lanham, Maryland 20706
http://www.rowmaneducation.com

Estover Road, Plymouth PL6 7PY, United Kingdom

British Library Cataloguing in Publication Information Available

Library of Congress Cataloging-in-Publication Data

Shapiro, Arthur S., 1928–
  Making large schools work : the advantages of small schools / Arthur Shapiro.
    p. cm.
  ISBN 978-1-60709-115-8 (cloth : alk. paper)—ISBN 978-1-60709-116-5 (pbk. :
alk. paper)—ISBN 978-1-60709-117-2 (electronic)
  1. School size—United States. 2. School improvement programs—United States.
I. Title.
  LB3012.5.S48 2008
  371.2'07—dc22   2009019936

Printed in the United States of America

™
∞ The paper used in this publication meets the minimum requirements of
American National Standard for Information Sciences—Permanence of Paper
for Printed Library Materials, ANSI/NISO Z39.48-1992.

Printed in the United States of America

It is because modern education is so seldom inspired by a great hope that it so seldom achieves great results.

—Bertrand Russell, *Why Men Fight*

Contents

Acknowledgments

"No man is an island . . ." said poet John Donne. When it comes to writing a book, nothing could be more true. This book could not have been in your hands without the dedicated and able contributions of:

Saundra Hart, whose good common sense and expertise with computers saved me from my flummoxes, poor formatting, and inability to construct tables and figures so they would be understandable. I truly appreciate her loyalty and hard work as a friend and a University Berbecker Scholarship Fellow.

Sue, my wife, patiently and with great insight, edited and made suggestions so that prose would be clear, relevant, and on target, all the while not wincing too much at my puns and quips.

A couple of my grad classes looked at the tables in the first two chapters, and thought they were clearer than mere text, so my uncertainty about starting out a book like this was allayed. Thanks muchly.

Lynne Menard, long-time friend and Berbecker Fellow, succinctly summarized the agonies teachers were suffering after reading the chapter about the issues and concerns elementary teachers faced when she said, "Help me. I'm drowning." Right on, Lynne.

It may amaze many of my closest and dearest friends and colleagues to read that I am not (yes, I repeat, not), a techie. So, to my techie friends and colleagues who, time after time rescue me from impending disaster, I say, muchas gracias to Susan Granda, Mike Ashley, and Kelly Fletcher.

Dedication

A dedication can tell one a good deal about the author, what kind of person he or she may be, how the author thinks, even provide a glimpse into what his/her values might be. Let's see how this plays out for you, the reader.

I dedicate this book to my family, who has given so much to enrich my life, my values, my thinking. Sue, my wife, partner, and editor, whose good, hard-nosed, and realistic common sense always comes through. One needs an editor like that. (It also helps to have wife like that—intuitive, who is also a mensch.) Our two children, Alana Shapiro-Thompson and Dr. Marc D. Shapiro, fit those criteria, both professional and thoughtful mensches as well. Their stimulating and penetrating thinking always contributes. I'm pretty lucky to have such a talented family.

Equally talented and insightful are my brother, Dr. Norman Shapiro, and his wife, Sandi. We are separated by space, but not by affection. This book can serve as a memorial to my long-time brilliant brother-in-law, Hal Linick, whom my adored and creative sister, Madeline, just lost. My wife credits Hal and Madeline with showing her what a partnership looks like.

Preface

HOW CAN THIS BOOK HELP US SOLVE THE TIDAL WAVE OF MAJOR PROBLEMS SINKING LARGE SCHOOLS?

In a small school, everyone is necessary.

—Stanton Leggett, Premier Educational Consultant

All things are created twice. First, mentally, and then physically. Building a house is the best example. It is created in every detail before the ground is even touched. When the physical creation begins, every decision is governed by the first (mental) creation.

—Stephen Corey

The purpose of this book is to lay out very practical approaches to making our ever-increasingly large schools work better—a lot better. American schools are undergoing huge changes, among the most significant of which is that their size is increasing rapidly. A couple of generations ago, Debra Meiers noted, most schools were quite small, about one hundred kids or so. Now, 70 percent of Americans attend high schools of one thousand or more kids, and almost 50 percent go to schools exceeding 1,500.

And large schools generate problems that make education much more difficult, such as:

- fosters and sustains the achievement gap,
- generates alienation,
- creates double the dropouts (at least),
- and poorer grades,
- greater security needs,
- meaning higher costs,
- and more (see chapter 1)

—unless we learn strategies to deal with such excessive size.

The best way to do this is to provide key practical research-based tools and strategies to pull this off.

This book digs away at the foreseen and unforeseen consequences of this rapid escalation of size, and presents practical, tried-and-true strategies for undoing some of the more unfortunate results of this social trend or drift. In other words, the book in section I first describes and analyzes some of the consequences of expanding size by comparing and contrasting the advantages and disadvantages of each in easy-to-read tables. Next, it explodes in a little over two pages the assumptions many of us believe favor large over small schools.

Reference Question

Do you want to hazard a guess regarding whether large or small schools generate more major negative results?

Section II provides us with *strategic tools* to understand our schools and how they operate. I say tools because, while most of us think of tools as physical objects (hammer, saw, computer, stethoscope), ideas and concepts can be extremely useful tools, which when properly understood and used, can make a huge difference in our daily lives. Think of a carpenter or a physician. Both need good tools with which to produce quality work. To do this, both need a clear mental picture, a clear vision of what quality work looks like before they start a project—or neither will be able to create it.

The physical tools are easy to see, but our mental tools are far more important, because they supply the vision of what could or should be. In education as well as in medicine, we need to be able to access our kit of diagnostic approaches or strategies to analyze the symptoms we uncover, and then develop antidotes (read, appropriate change strategies) to deal with the issues and concerns we face.

Mental models, then, are educators' tools to change our systems. Without them we are mere tinkerers—doomed to fritter away fruitlessly at the edges of our challenges.

So, chapter 3 in section II deals with how schools as organizations operate—their dynamics—so that practitioners can understand what they are dealing with. We look at how to create a healthy subculture based on roles, role expectations, and how norms and subcultures are and can be developed. In chapter 4 we then examine different *metaphors* or *images* of organizations that surround us that may, and often do, influence our thinking and consequent behavior without our even realizing it. And we present a Curriculum-Steering Committee structure and process which *generates curriculum change to renew the school as a routine*, a relatively novel idea and practice in light of the fact that all organizations (including schools) are entropic, meaning they decay.

In chapter 5, we describe, analyze, and predict the exact, but the subtle and hidden, effects of the major *pulls* the five parts of organizations exert that often confound and surprise us. For example, note our top echelon's persistent mission to centralize all decision making.

In the succeeding chapter 6, we describe, analyze, and predict the exact sequence of the *three phases in their careers* that each of our organizations inevitably careens through uncontrollably, which generally ends with a too-long phase of bureaucratic slumber, doing nothing while the organization slowly deteriorates (such as General Motors and Chrysler). We also suggest how to defeat this inevitable outcome.

Next to last, in this section, chapter 7, we deal briefly with the eternal issue of *power* (any decent book on schools and organizations must deal with power to help us avoid screwing up) and last, chapter 8 looks at *leadership* from the perspective of a social force that can be used constructively. If people involved in change do not grasp organizational dynamics, their most sincere efforts can and often do blow up in their faces.

In chapter 9 in section III, we lay out *several change strategies* and then the key bottom-up strategy I used to decentralize large elementary, middle, and high schools, called the *Analysis of the Dynamics of Organizational Change*.

In section IV we provide a chapter on each of the actual effective and practical step-by-step, blow-by-blow *diagrams* of the strategies used to decentralize first a junior high, chapter 10, into a model middle school. The next two chapters, 11 and 12, take us into the decentralizing strategies and processes that drove a so-so elementary school to become the premier model for the region, a school with a constructivist philosophy and matching teaching practices. Chapter 13 is the saga of the least effective high school with the most minority students of seventeen high schools in a large district becoming the high school with the greatest improvement academically, as well as in a number of other dimensions. With all three schools, we were able to pull this off successfully despite all sorts of obstacles, as surfaced in the issues and concerns people reported that they faced.

And last in section V, in chapter 14, we sum up and concretely delineate four *internal structures* necessary not only to pull off decentralization, but also to maintain and to improve it over time. One fully described in chapter 4 illustrates how *to make change a routine* through the vehicle of a *Curriculum-Steering Task Force* to keep the organization viable over long periods of time. The processes and structures to move into *Small Learning Communities (SLCs) and Professional Learning Communities (PLCs)* are described and analyzed in chapters 10, 11, 12, and 13, as is the fourth structure, establishing a *Planning Task Force* that works.

I

SIZE GENERATES SHOALS
THAT CAN WRECK US

Small schools cut poverty's power over achievement by 80 to 90 percent
in reading, writing, and mathematics.

—Bickel and Howley, *The Influence of Scale*

If you really want to increase test scores (and presumably, learning) in
low-achieving schools with high levels of poverty . . . Just reduce the size
of the student body.

—Paul Abramson, Educational Consultant and Editor

1

Size *Really* Matters

A Sea of Troubles (Why Do We Have Problems Making Large Schools Work?) Comparing and Contrasting Large and Small Schools

We can develop a good large school, but it's much harder to do than in a small school.

—Stanton Leggett, educational consultant

ARE OUR SCHOOLS TOO LARGE?

A funny thing is happening on the road to education: our schools got very big—no, huge.

Approximately 70 percent of high school students in America go to schools with one thousand or more kids. And almost 50 percent go to schools with over 1,500. Schools of 2,200 and more are common. Deborah Meier recently noted (2006) that when she was born, there were two hundred thousand school districts (now, under fifteen thousand) and most schools had about one hundred kids enrolled. We can thank James Conant (1959), former president of Harvard, for supplying the rationale to eliminate small schools and increase their size to provide a larger, comprehensive program of courses.

But, does it have consequences!

Reflective Question

So, why is this important? What does large size buy us?

Well, it isn't very good for our kids, teachers, school leaders—or our communities.

Evidence? How about just a few highlights (more shortly):

- Supports the achievement gap. (Surprised?)
- Do you want to encourage kids to drop out? Just put two thousand kids into a school. Do you know what that does? It *generates twice* as many dropouts as in a school of six hundred.
- What does it do to principals? It forces them to become firemen rushing around to put out blazes.
- Achievement? Actually depresses it.
- Safety? Less safe.
- Attend classes? My wife ran a small diner, missed forty-eight of ninety days one semester—and still passed.
- *South of Heaven's* (1993) author, Thomas French, reports one kid never attended class, wandered the halls all day for an entire year—and got away with it.

OK, let's compare and contrast small (one hundred to four hundred or five hundred) and large schools. Then, in chapters 3 through 7, we'll take a look at the dynamics organizations generate, and in the first chapter, we'll examine the reasons that cause these results.

Obviously, both large and small schools have advantages and disadvantages. Inquiring into the differences as well as the advantages and disadvantages between large and small schools requires us to focus on key components of schools, and the process and structure of schooling. We'll use tables, since they're a quick and visual way to summarize these key components by comparing and contrasting differences.

At the end of the tables, let's decide which is more advantageous. (Obviously, a major thrust of this book is to decentralize large schools into smaller internal units.) Table 1.1 deals with the "indispensable elements," as Barnard (1938), the father of administrative thought, called them, of any organization. That includes schools, the U.S. Marines, local stores, corporations, even our families.

OK, we've nailed down these absolute essentials to any organization:

- Purpose
- Cooperation
- Communication

Table 1.1. Advantages and Disadvantages of Large and Small Schools

Component	Large	Small
I. Purpose		
Barnard (1939) notes *three indispensable elements* of an organization: Purpose is the first. A clear sense of mission is a criterion for an "effective school."	If we have a large student body, we need a large faculty. Informal means of sharing information is limited. People interact primarily with their depts. or grade levels or teams. Shared sense of school purpose is lost (Oxley, 1989, p. 29).	Faculty *and* students can develop a shared sense of purpose. Since people feel they belong, they buy into goals, developing a greater sense of participating and belonging.
II. Cooperation		
The second of Barnard's indispensable elements of any organization. Obviously, an organization (including our family) cannot build a shared purpose unless people cooperate to achieve it.	Cooperation is harder to develop when people are further from source(s) of power. Departments, grades, or teams become the fulcrums around which people hang their loyalties and efforts.	People cooperate more easily in small enterprises. We feel close to each other *and* feel important *because everyone is needed.*
III. Communication		
Barnard's third indispensable element is essential to communicate purposes and for people to cooperate in achieving purposes. Without communication, we wander in all directions, because coordination becomes impossible.	Communication in large organizations becomes top-down. The overall communications system becomes formal. Going through the channels, which become hierarchical, is difficult—and sometimes dangerous, so most people give up. So, purpose and cooperation tend to become lost. We interact within our own formal and informal structures.	Communication is simpler and faster. Information is an informal basis so that everyone becomes informed, usually rapidly. The organization becomes a *small face-to-face folk society*—in which everyone knows and recognizes everyone.
	Generally, students are excluded, becoming merely bystanders.	Students can become part of this.
Lines of communication	Generally long, which can generate difficulties in communicating.	Can be short and direct—therefore, more effective.

The next table compares and contrasts student achievement and graduation rates in small and large schools. In this day and age of our testing mania (terminology courtesy of psychologist and *Phi Delta Kappan* columnist Gerald Bracey), it becomes essential to analyze size of school objectively and thoughtfully. Table 1.2 also deals with poverty and the achievement gap and with the way schools are organized, as well as their structure.

So far, so good. Using tables to compare and to contrast gives us a quick visual scan of the advantages of small schools. They pop out. How about a startling conclusion about the huge amount of literature regarding the achievement gap? *If you want to reduce it, decentralize into small learning communities (SLCs).*

Now, let's look at how size impacts creating healthy or unhealthy school climates and cultures. Consequently, table 1.3 compares and contrasts behavior and relationships that are also impacted by school size. (A warning: we won't like the comparison if we inhabit large schools.) The table also compares trust/distrust, the emotional support generated by school size.

I find myself amazed at the impact of large and small size on schools and schooling. As we read on, we next deal with governance, discipline, and accountability (which have become third rails in the United States and the UK), and with the roles of the principal players in schools: leadership, teachers, and students. (Disclosure: I taught in a school of five thousand boys and was a principal in a high school of 325 students [but it took me a while to begin to think about and to understand the effect of scale in organizations.])

Table 1.5 deals with the program, that is, the curriculum of the school, as well as other outcomes, some of which may be considered essential to our society and culture (such as taking responsibility, making wise decisions and wise use of time, developing strong personal locus of control, even retaining teachers). Costs will be treated in table 1.6, the last in this chapter.

How are we doing? Convinced?

Table 1.2.

	Large	*Small*
IV. Student Achievement, Graduation Rate, Attendance, Violence		
	Generates decreased student achievement, lower graduation rates and attendance, more violence.	Eckman & Howley (1997) ". . . found a strong relationship between higher academic achievement and lower enrollment."
		A recent research summary by USDOE . . . notes the value of small schools in increasing achievement, graduation rates, satisfaction, and in improving behavior has been "confirmed with a clarity and level of confidence rare in the annals of education research" (Raywid, 1999).
		Greater academic achievement (Fowler& Walberg, 1991).
	Since relational trust is reduced, achievement is reduced (Bryk & Schneider, 2002).	With increased relational trust, achievement rises.
		The Chicago Public Schools study found: Student performance and test scores improved,
		Violence occurred less frequently,
		Conditions were more conducive for students to learn and for teachers to develop professionally, . . . (Wasley, et al., 2000).
		"More academically productive" (Lee & Smith, 1997; Lee, Smith, & Croninger, 1997, April) "Better behaved" (Godfredson, 1985).

(continued)

Table 1.2. (*Continued*)

	Large	*Small*
A. Poverty **The Achievement Gap**	"The correlation between poverty and low achievement can be as high as 10 times stronger" (Eckman & Howley, 1997). "... small schools cut poverty's power over achievement by 80 to 90 percent in reading, writing, and mathematics" (Bickel & Howley, 2002, March). "If you really want to increase test scores (and, presumably, learning) in low-achieving schools with high levels of poverty . . . just reduce the size of the student body" (Abramson, 2000, May).	Benefits not limited to low income communities. Greater equity in achievement (Lee & Smith, 1995). Achievement gap reduced.
	Usually little involvement of parents and community. More difficult to do with social distance operating. Students feel distant from principals, teachers, each other.	Parents can be considerably more involved in a small school— and, often are. Wasley et al. (2000) found that "parents and community members were satisfied with the school." "Small schools created out of large schools in Chicago have been a successful means of involving students, parents, and teachers in the process of educational reform" (Nathan & Febey, 2001).

	Large	Small
V. Organization and Structure		
Much variation from centralized to decentralized; whole school; grade-level; small school or small learning community; departmentalized; interdisciplinary team, etc.	More formal. A more elaborate administrative hierarchy becomes necessary. People are more distant from each other. Social distance is greater. In secondary schools, departments usually emerge, automatically creating social distance.	More informal. All players (administrators, teachers, students, parents) are closer. They know each other. Departments are unnecessary. SLC structure gives teachers flexibility to tailor instruction to their students' needs.

Table 1.3.

	Large	Small
VI. Climate and Culture		

VI. Climate and Culture

"*Climate* is to the organization what personality is to the individual." (Halpin & Croft, 1963).

Culture can be considered shared, learned behavior that people learn in social living. These are the customs, norms, expectations people develop of each other.

Roles also become a major aspect, as are expectations people in their roles develop of each other.

Large

Generally greater *social distance*, far less trust. "Students are more remote from staff; they rely on their own friendship circles for support. A strong, shared sense of community does not exist between staff and students or even among the students. It is not difficult to understand why destructive student sub-cultures often emerge." (Oxley, 1989, p. 28). Students become more polarized, small active group of participants and a large number of non-participants. (Just look into the frequency of participation listed for kids in yearbooks to get a sense of this.)

Reduced opportunity for ownership to develop. Reduced sense to develop a stake in the school.

Harder to develop sense of identity in a depersonalized atmosphere.

Social climate, particularly in lower socio-economic areas, unfavorable for learning—produces poorer attendance, class cutting, dropping out, non-involvement in extra-curricular activities, and more . . . vandalism and violence are the norm. (Oxley, 1989, p. 28).

Small

Close social distance (people feel part of the operation of the school). Much more trust generally. Possibility for greater inclusion of students. Greater flexibility. More chance for informality.

Much greater *participation*: three to twenty times greater in certain extracurricular activities, such as participating in district music festivals, dramatic, journalistic, student government competitions; twice as great in average number of extracurricular activities (Barker & Gump, 1964).

Greater *sense of ownership*. Leads to developing a stake in the school. Student, teacher *satisfaction* much greater, since *everyone is needed*.

Sense of identity with school developed.

". . . smaller high schools are more engaging environments and produce greater gains in student achievement . . . a now large body of research provides evidence that smaller schools are more productive work places for both adults and students. In these more intimate environments,

Large	Small

		teachers are more likely to report greater satisfaction with their work, higher levels of morale, and greater commitment. Problems of student misconduct, class cutting, absenteeism, and dropping out are all less prevalent (Bryk et al., 1994: 6-7).

A. Behavior—Relationships

Establishing *relationships* with each other for students and teachers is essential. Many people *need* relationships to be healthy emotionally.	Social distance marked. Students, even teachers often anonymous, depersonalized. Many kids who are marginal become alienated because they cannot establish positive relationships.	Personalized, sense of community easy to establish. Essentially a folk community with face-to-face contact daily with each other. "We're like a family."
	Above 500 students, teachers and administrators do not know all kids by name. Beyond 1,000, they cannot distinguish an intruder from a student (Oxley, 1989, p. 28). In large schools, teachers do not know each other.	Teachers, kids, administrators know everyone.
Are students *connected* with each other, with teachers?	Greater difficulty in students becoming connected with each other, with teachers. Greater dissatisfaction.	Much easier to establish connections, since students needed to run the school. More opportunity to create satisfactory relationships.

B. Trust—distrust

Trust essential for effective human relationships and leadership.	Trust more difficult to establish when social distance exists. Need direct intervention with trust-building exercises, and still difficult.	Much easier to establish when we know everyone. Good idea to develop trust-building exercises to remind everyone of its necessity.
Relational trust, grounded in social respect and personal regard, crucial (Bryk & Schneider, 2002).	Relational trust more difficult to develop.	Relational trust easier to develop. Higher academic achievement occurs

(continued)

Table 1.3. *(Continued)*

	Large	*Small*
		with higher relational trust (Bryk & Schneider, 2002).
C. Emotional Support for Teachers, Kids Professional Learning Communities (PLCs) can facilitate this.	Harder to develop.	Easier to pull off. Teacher support improved (Cotton, 2001).
D. Conflict and Conflict Resolution	Greater opportunity for conflict to remain unresolved. Poisons climate.	Can deal with conflict more readily with trust and acceptance.
E. School as a Community The internal community. "The sense that each person belongs to a group and feels some commitment to it, that each is responsible to the others for his/her actions." (Gregory & Smith, 1987, p. 261).	"A strong, shared sense of community does not exist between staff and students or even among students." (Oxley, p. 28). The large size of the high school, once considered its strength, has become a major handicap. It has become a difficult institution for people to commit to or identify with." (Gregory & Smith, 1987, p. 5). In large organizations, informal organizations (social systems) make living in the organization more satisfying. Informal organizations set boundaries to separate people from the organization. Little identification of the individual with the total faculty.	Strong sense of community can develop. High level of identification with the school. Virtually no "outsiders" are generated (those students who have poor academic records, no or few extracurricular involvement and who lose their connections with the school). The small school doesn't alienate as many or any students.

Table 1.4.

	Large	*Small*
VII. Governance		
How is consent obtained?	Authority structure imposed.	Emerges from "community" interaction.
How are authority and power distributed and how are decisions made?	Heavy emphasis on control and order. Control is external. Student Council often principal's pawns. Decision-making often top-down.	Often full teacher involvement. Often full student involvement since everyone is needed, providing teachers and students a heightened sense of their own efficacy, and self-esteem. Teachers, students can be more involved in policy-making. Greater sense of trust.
A. Discipline and Control	External. Social controls often minimized. Faculty often fragmented. Strong focus on control, limitations. But students often wander in halls in high schools (French, 1993). Students typically excluded, so control is imposed.	Internal controls expected. Social controls effective. Faculty often can be unified. A democratic governance model can emerge. Principal can more readily share power with faculty *and* students. "Small schools are more orderly and have more social controls operating. In part, this is due to everyone knowing everyone, something that is impossible in a large school" (Leggett & Shapiro, 1983). Less student disorder and violence (Garbarino, 1978; Godfredson, 1985).
B. Accountability	Can be blurred in the bureaucracy.	Very clear. The failure of any component is clearly visible (Leggett, Brubaker, Cohodes & Shapiro, 1977).

(*continued*)

Table 1.4. *(Continued)*

	Large	Small
C. Role of principal	Principal more distant, can be more isolated. More of an authority figure. Can hide behind formalities, develop ceremonies. Function as firemen to put out fires. Develop crisis mentality.	Principal can take role of head teacher. Authority barrier tends to become removed. All components visible; hard to hide things. Primacy of control issues can end. Improved instructional leadership (Wasley et al., 2000).
D. Role of teacher	Teacher becomes primary control agent. Causes student-teacher relationship to erode.	Students can become primary control agents because everything is so visible. Freedom gives teachers and students opportunity to build strong, supportive relationships. Trust permits teachers and students to identify more easily with the school. Functional support systems for teachers and students can emerge, since teachers are more easily able to relate more effectively with personal concerns of kids.
	Usually feel powerless, pawns.	Feel more effective, can have greater autonomy, and thus, feel more powerful.
	Staff more specialized (more foreign languages, science specialties). Departments become basic units in secondary schools.	Staff must be generalists, unless large school subdivides. Faculty can plan as total group. Have to be more flexible. Often come off as learners. Often perceived as knowledgeable.
	Teacher and student satisfaction usually less.	Greater teacher and student satisfaction.

	Large	Small
E. Role of student		
	Students separated from faculty. Cliques often form to protect individuals against the organization because they feel powerless.	Student-teacher contact maximized, producing more effective relationships with each other. Teachers get to know students, and visa versa; no one is a stranger. Students get to know principal. Everyone is needed, thus feels more valuable. Greater emotional support provided. What kids are like makes a difference. Greater satisfaction with school, peers.
	Students passive, e.g., rarely take initiative in developing curriculum, passive role in governance. Students discouraged from involvement, growth.	Student roles expanded. Can be proactive. Student needs can be met better.
	Little support of democratic beliefs, procedures. Often set up competition among students, teachers. Internal school dynamics produce students who feel alienated, left out— often act out.	Cooperation enhanced. "Students develop a higher sense of satisfaction with: a. physical well-being b. acquiring knowledge c. developing intellectual interests—they can more easily identify with a teacher d. developing a healthy self-concept—mutual respect generates this e. they have more opportunities f. having more important, responsible positions g. developing a sense of confidence (Shapiro, Benjamin, & Hunt, 1995).

Table 1.5.

	Large	*Small*
VIII. Program/curriculum	Can be large, specialized. But, only 12% take these specialized courses. ". . . an expanded, more specialized, more diversified curriculum is not guaranteed by large enrollment levels alone" (Monk, 1987, pp. 11–12).	Can be huge (Leggett, et al., 1977). Cannot have large-scale football, cheerleading, if working with one small school. If decentralize a large school, can pull this off.
	High structure limits time for students, faculty to meet informally.	More opportunity for teachers, students to meet informally.
	"The quality of instruction is the most important determinant of student achievement and has no relationship to the number of courses offered" (Eckman & Howley, 1997).	Interdisciplinary collaboration and consensus greater (Oxley, 1997b). Greater program coordination (Wasley et al., 2000).
IX. Other outcomes		
A. For students		
1. Responsibility	Faculty concerned to provide external direction to students.	Can learn to be responsible for own decisions, actions.
2. Freedom	Self-direction not a focus.	Can learn to be autonomous.
	Students generally perceived as unable to handle freedom and responsibility.	Can learn what freedom means—and how to use it.
3. Wise decision-making	More difficult, since little opportunity provided.	Can learn to make wise decisions, since wider latitude for student decision-making.
4. Respect	Generally not respected to take responsibility.	Are respected as people, so can learn to respect others.
5. Make wise use of time	Little opportunity within tighter constraints for opportunity to practice.	Can learn since more opportunity to make decisions.

	Large	*Small*
6. Participation in school activities		Three to 20 times greater participation (Barker & Gump, 1964). More likely to participate in school activities (Lindsey, 1982; Pittman & Haughwout, 1987)
B. For the school		
1. Generating dropouts	Large schools with over 2,000 produce twice the percentage of dropouts of schools with 600 or less. Generally more rigid.	Reduced dropouts because little opportunity for kids to become alienated. "Less likely to drop out of school" (Pittman & Haughwout, 1987; Lindsey, 1982).
2. Uses of time	External for students, faculty. Little autonomy in decision-making.	Can be much more flexible.
3. Locus of control	Tends to be external.	Internal. Considerable to great autonomy.
4. Diversity	A function of board policy.	The same.
5. Retaining teachers		". . . teachers in small schools are much more satisfied. . . . (Bryk, 1994; Wasley et al, 2000; Raywid, 1996). ". . . the single most effective way to retain teachers" in a study of urban, rural, suburban superintendents (Hare, et al., 2001).

Table 1.6.

	Large	*Small*
X. Costs	Economies of scale one of two rationales for consolidating small schools. ". . . empirical evidence for cost savings only apply to very small schools" (Walberg & Fowler, 1987) and "only if achievement and other positive schooling outcomes are not considered" (Fowler & Walberg, 1991). "With regard to the supposed economy of scale, much of it results from providing proportionately fewer support staff and extracurricular activities, and providing less space for these items. However, these savings also represent costs in terms of dropout rates, poor attendance, vandalism, etc. If the financial costs associated with the negative effects of larger schools were accounted for, any economy of scale probably would not be evident" (Oxley, 1989, p. 28).	High tech, AV is more costly, but small schools can be cost-effective. It costs little more if any at all, if the teaching system changes (Leggett, Brubaker, Cohodes & Shapiro, 1977, p. 56).

CONCLUSION?

OK, which is more advantageous? A slam dunk.

IMPORTANT TERMS

Climate—climate is to the organization as personality is to the individual (Halpin 1966).

Culture—shared, learned behavior that people learn in social living (Linton 1955).

Relational trust—based on social respect and personal regard people have for each other (Bryk and Schneider 2002).

Social distance—people's willingness to engage in close social contacts or relationships of varying degrees of closeness with those in diverse social groups, such as racial, ethnic, and other groups (Bogardus' Social Distance Scale [1926]).

2

Our Assumptions and Beliefs Drive Us

We Hardly Realize What They Are— and That They Do

A belief is a lever that, once pulled, moves almost everything else in a person's life.

—Sam Harris, *The End of Faith*

SO, LET'S LOOK AT OUR ASSUMPTIONS AND BELIEFS ABOUT LARGE AND SMALL SCHOOLS

A point illustrates this. I was making a few brief (mercifully) comments to a PTA group, and I heard myself say, "Well, knowledge has to be useful, you know."

It absolutely stopped me dead. Here I was stating an assumption that I deeply believed that I never had been aware of. Incidentally, I was taking a course in educational philosophy at the time, which Dr. Dunkel later called "Starting Points." He illustrated why he changed the title because of an example of the way beliefs drive our behavior.

When curtains in a room catch fire, some people will say, "How can I get out of here?" And they'll bolt.

Others will ask, "How can I put it out?" They'll pull the curtains down and stamp it out. Still others (bureaucrats, or, maybe, social workers) will ask, "How can we get consensus on putting this out?" So, they'll call a meeting.

(OK, OK, that's a joke.)

But look at what our hidden assumptions, our beliefs, (our starting points), do. Simply, they drive our action. The reason for thinking about this in a book on decentralizing large schools seems clear. The research on the benefits of small school size is pretty clear—and has been so, increasingly, for three decades. So why do we keep on building larger and larger schools? Our hidden beliefs, our hidden assumptions drive us.

People simply believe that large schools are better.

Reflective Questions

Do you? If so, why?

OK, let's take a very brief look at these assumptions with a short table—a *very* short table.

Conclusions? You make them.

Table 2.1.

Assumption/Belief	Large	Small
Bigger is better.	Favors the large school.	Research in chapter 1 refutes this.
A large school looks more substantial, gives people a greater sense of confidence.	It does.	People may feel uneasy about the small size, informality.
Large schools can meet student needs better.	See tables in chapter 1. They do not.	
Achievement— kids can get a better education, learn more, test better.	Research contradicts this. Generates decreased student achievement (Cotton, 1996).	Student performance and test scores improved (Wasley et al., 2000).
Graduation rates are better.	No, poorer.	Higher.
Large size means more efficiency.	Beyond 1,200 students, high schools need more security, bigger halls for more kids.	Small can be more efficient (except for very small schools).
Accountability	Teachers, administrators, kids can hide. Ceremonies can obscure responsibility.	Everyone, everything is highly visible. Kids have to be where they're supposed to be.
Effectiveness	Much less. Much harder to develop a good large school.	Considerably more effective (Wasley et al., 2000).
Relationships among teachers, kids, and leadership	Much harder to pull off.	Much easier to develop. Faculty can stay with kids 3-4 years.
Competence of faculty	Teachers can be specialists (physics teachers, orchestra directors).	Are generalists; in a decentralized large school will have specialists.
Greater variety of courses	Conant (1959) advocated large high schools to provide large number of courses. Most kids do not take them.	Can offer a "huge variety of programs, based on and tailored to needs of the students..." (Leggett, Brubaker, Cohodes & Shapiro, 1977, p. 56).
Safety	People more anonymous, so safety sacrificed.	Greater.
Satisfaction	Less.	More.
Leadership	Principals can be executives, great for one's ego.	Very visible. Can be more effective.
Supervision	Supervision based on developing a trusting relationship, so not as effective.	Can be very effective, since have contact daily; can build trust, relationships.
Autonomy (highly prized by teachers, leadership)	Can have autonomy since can be unnoticed.	Can be great.

II

HOW ORGANIZATIONS (READ SCHOOLS) WORK—THEIR DYNAMICS

If you want truly to understand something, try to change it.

—Kurt Lewin

The responsibility of a leader is to define reality.

—Max DePree, *The Art of Leadership*

3

How to Make Sure We Stay Afloat (How to Work with the Dynamics of the School, So We Don't Screw Up Too Badly) and How to Create a Healthy Subculture in the Process

Some kids know how to operate in organizations, and some kids have no idea of what to do and how to do it. So they can't avoid getting into trouble—so they become victims.

—Alana and Marc Shapiro, when they were teenagers

INTRODUCTION

Reflective Questions

1. Why should we in leadership study how organizations function?
2. Don't we know that?

If we do not understand thoroughly how organizations function, we will succeed in running them only by being really lucky. And who can count on luck to bail us out all the time? To put it starkly, we cannot be successful without understanding *how organizations operate*. Some tragic, career-destroying examples exist of principals forgetting this in their haste to move rapidly once they assume that they hold the reins of power.

Actually, we live, we swim in a sea, an ocean, of organizations virtually every day, every hour, and every minute of our lives. We are awakened by a radio broadcasting from a station (an organization), we eat cereal manufactured and distributed by organizations, we listen to an organization (the police) informing us of traffic jams on our way to work in our organization's building, we drive there in a car built by another organization, serviced by an organization. . . . So even our day starts with numerous organizations, some subtly and others directly, impacting us.

This chapter deals with some universal and major aspects of the *structure of organizations*, including *positions, roles, role expectations*, and their *virtually inevitable conflict* because we occupy a variety of roles in our personal and professional lives. We also deal with such factors as *hierarchy* and *authority*, coming up with some startling insights, which are extremely important for us to function effectively in our organizational lives.

Next, we deal with another major universal component of the structure of organizations. Namely, we inevitably create *social systems (groups), which are guided by customs or norms we can help create,* and a *subculture and climate* as we live in our organizations.

Next comes chapter 4, "Hidden Eddies That Can Drive Us Off Course: Metaphors and Images of Organizations (That Often Dominate Our Thinking)," of which we are virtually unaware and that drive our behavior. This is followed by chapter 5, "Five Hidden Whirlpools (*Pulls*, or Centers of Influence) That the Five Parts of the Organization Inevitably Generate," again, which seem to slip by our awareness and which drive the organization in supposedly irrational directions.

A KEY UNIVERSAL ELEMENT: STRUCTURE

Reflective Questions

1. Have you ever sat back and asked what key elements every organization in our society displays, even the informal ones like families and friendship groups?
2. What are they?

If we examine organizations very carefully, we see that they are man-made entities. As a matter of fact, sociologists consider them *socially constructed realities*—for example, one of the things we do in organizations when they start is to create structures immediately.

If you bet that all organizations develop a structure, even as they start, you can take your winnings to the bank. Just look at organizations—any one. Your school has a principal, teachers, students, custodians, perhaps cafeteria workers, and if large enough, an assistant principal or two, often a counselor. And let's not forget the students, who develop student councils, honor societies, clubs, teams, and on and on.

The U.S. Navy has a structure (admirals, captains, ensigns, chiefs, seamen), as do our local stores (manager, clerks), and the local library. So do the U.S. Marines, as does the local church, temple, or synagogue (minister or priest or rabbi, secretary, members, president of the parishioners, etc.). Whenever I go into an organization, I want to know the structure, since it tells me who is responsible to whom, which is crucial in working effectively with any organization.

Reflective Question

Now, what do you think are the universal elements of these organizational structures?

UNIVERSAL ELEMENTS: ALL ORGANIZATIONS CREATE POSITIONS AND ROLES: THEIR BUILDING BLOCKS

Charlie Brown as Manager and Pitcher—and Loser

When any organization is created, we think immediately of different *positions* necessary to run it. When Charlie Brown gets his baseball team together, he always takes the manager's position (where he manages to create his role as a wimp); at the same time, he sets up his role as pitcher, too—another position. And the different characters literally take different positions (outfielder, first baseman). If a restaurant opens up near you, it always has a manager, cooks, usually cashiers and servers, and you, the customer.

Even informal organizations, such as our families or clubs, create positions. Two adults can create a family. When and if children arrive, they occupy considerably different positions from adults. Grandparents have different positions from parents, different from uncles and aunts.

Sociologists also call positions *statuses*, which differs from *prestige*. Prestige is allocated in different amounts to various positions. Obviously, ministers have more prestige than choirboys and choir directors, as does the principal in comparison with teachers, and they, in turn, with their pupils. The ship's captain has much more prestige in that position than deckhands.

The next critical element is the *role*. A role consists of a *series of expectations* for a position—any position (Gross, Mason, and McEachern 1966). And expectations differ, so that one can be a passive, laissez-faire principal, another person can act out his role as a bureaucrat, still another as a faculty or student advocate, and still another principal can develop a different set of expectations as . . . (you fill this in). The point is that roles for positions can differ according to various expectations different groups develop for that status, as well as those that the person in the position develops.

Thus, *how* a person acts out a status becomes that person's role. Charlie Brown creates a hapless role as a manager. As a football kicker, his role invariably is that of a sucker for Lucy. Lucy always takes the role of the wiseass. Interestingly, both their roles are fairly stable, generally true of roles people develop and sustain. Note, then, that the role we develop consists of our understanding and acting out of one series of the expectations surrounding it. It comprises our *interpretation* of how that position should be implemented. Others might carry them out quite differently.

INTERESTINGLY, AS ROLE EXPECTATIONS DEVELOP, THEY CAN CREATE ROLE CONFLICT

Charlie Brown and Phil Jackson

It is pretty obvious that different clusters of role expectations can develop for each position. While Charlie Brown expects to be an inept manager (and pitcher, too), Phil Jackson, formerly manager of the World Champion Chicago Bulls and then of the Los Angeles Lakers basketball teams, functioned quite differently. He expected his teams to win. A novelty among coaches, his interpretation bordered on a Zen role. I once saw a coach being highly stressed out, and remarked to a dean who had been a former coach that the man on TV was so wild. The dean noted, "That's his choice."

For principals, a series of different role expectations can be seen—and, sometimes heard, often according to which important reference group you focus on.

- Superintendents want reports in on time, which is their expectation for a principal's role.
- Most teachers want to be treated with consideration and compassion.
- Often, parents want control, and their kids to get high test scores.
- The union does not want teachers to be hassled.
- A principal is expected by fellow principals to look, dress, and act confidently.
- The Board of Education wants principals to look professional, to follow policies, and to keep order.

Reference Groups/Social Systems and Role Conflict—Not Funny

Each of these groups is essentially a *reference group*, or a *social system*, toward which principals have to keep a weather eye to satisfy them. It sometimes is a tall order, to which any principal can attest. And therein lies the rub.

The principal new to the role has to tack through the various conceptions of the role to survive—let alone prosper, often a difficult proposition. My comments above regarding each reference group's or social system's expectations are somewhat simplified, since reference groups often develop a variety of expectations, often conflicting, among their members to define the role of the principal.

Thus, role expectations take time to ferret out as one lives in organizations. People from the outside often are unaware of the welter of conflicting expectations from each social system, a reason why administrators with no experience as teachers or administrators so often fail. They fail to pick up the riptides, the underwater currents, the hidden shoals of expectations that each social system holds for leaders. And failure to pick up on those undercurrents can lead to severe disappointments to key social systems—even loss of their support.

Examples abound. Sometimes, new teachers may expect principals to help them with their organization or with the discipline of classes, and may approach principals openly and trustingly. More veteran teachers, possibly burned by previous administrators, do not want to draw attention to themselves, may distrust the principal, and keep their distance warily (both social and spatial), waiting to see how the principal operates. We will deal with the absolutely crucial role of trust and distrust in chapter 8. Some teachers may want principals to treat everyone equally, while others may want differential treatment (being able to take time to take care of their kids, to go to a physician or dentist during school hours). These provide administrators with crisp examples of role conflict.

As for parents, some may want their kids to be treated as special (National Honor Society or elite advanced, ability-grouped classes [particularly true of upper-middle-class parents]), while others may want all kids to be treated alike and not have to contend with fallout from tracking. So life for principals is not a bowl of cherries. Note that teachers also develop widely differing expectations for such issues as ability grouping and tracking.

GETZELS' AND GUBA'S CONTRIBUTIONS TO UNDERSTANDING ROLE CONFLICT

So different expectations arise from the same social system or reference group. Getzels and Guba (1957) addressed this in their famous model, later modified by Thelen (Getzels and Thelen 1960) (see figure 3.1). Observing people interacting in organizations, they saw two dimensions of behavior. The first, the *nomothetic*, consists of the organization developing various roles, illustrated by clusters of expectations, which are developed to achieve the organization's goals. The second, Getzels and Guba called the

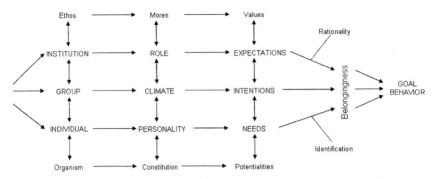

Figure 3.1.   Getzel and Guba's Social Behavior and Administrative Process

Source: J. W. Getzels and H. A. Thelen, "The classroom group as a unique social system," *Yearbook of the National Society for the Study of Education* 59, no. 2 (1960): 53–82.

idiographic dimension, consisting of the individual's personality predispositions, which consist of individual's needs.

Getzels and Guba, in their effort to understand how individuals and organizations operate, stated, "To understand the behavior of specific role incumbents in an institution, we must know both the role-expectations and the need-dispositions. Indeed, needs and expectations may be thought of as motives for behavior, the one driving from personal propensities, the other from institutional requirements." Later, they added, "A given act is conceived as deriving simultaneously from both the nomothetic and the idiographic dimensions. . . . (S)ocial behavior results as the individual attempts to cope with the environment composed of patterns of expectations for his behavior in ways consistent with his own independent patterns of needs" (1957, 52–54).

INTERPRETATION: MY CONFLICTING
INTERNAL EXPECTATIONS FOR MY ROLE

OK, what are they saying?

The value of this model is that it points out conflict that may occur in any person and in any organization caused by different expectations we have for roles personally and professionally. A principal may want to be caring, yet has to evaluate teachers doing a poor job, failing to meet his or her own expectations for the position. These are conflicting role expectations each person may hold.

"Tough love" provides a crystal clear example of role conflict by a person who faces the trauma of turning a child over to the police for illegal drug use and yet desperately loves the child. What to do? This illustrates the pain any of us who enables someone may face. We suddenly realize that our behavior is essentially crippling the person by permitting the continuation of dysfunctional behavior.

In actuality, extreme forms of internal role conflict within oneself are the stuff of high drama, although rare. When Mark Anthony sees Cleopatra fleeing the battlefield at Actium, he is torn as to whether to follow her or not. He follows her, abandoning his fleet and troops. Since he abandons them, they in turn feel it is appropriate to abandon him. His two horrendously conflicting roles (lover and general) come into conflict.

INTERPRETATION: MY VARIOUS ROLES IN CONFLICT

Reflective Questions

1. What role conflicts do you face in your professional practice?
2. Which are conflicts among the various roles you play?

Next, we can look at conflicting expectations faced by principals in their organizational roles. Principals may want to be perceived by their own personal kids as caring and loving, and yet have role expectations to have high expectations for performance for secretaries and teachers, and may have to replace them. We see these two roles in conflict.

We next can view role expectations from two different social systems. The faculty might expect the principal to suspend the football team's seventeen-year-old honor student kicker for drinking beer on a skiing trip (the principal's rule-enforcing role), while the parents might want a more merciful decision—and threaten legal action for suspension. It can get even more complicated when the principal realizes that suspending the student might cause the team to lose the game with a fellow principal's team, with whom there is a friendly bet about wearing that team's jersey in school the next Monday if the team lost.

We often are caught between a number of not-so-obvious conflicting expectations, which Getzels and Guba clearly pointed out.

For example, of late, the high-stakes testing mania has placed many between the grinding teeth of wanting their kids to do well, and the ethical necessity of letting happen what may happen. Some teachers have tried to help their students, destroying their teaching careers.

Other illustrations may help us understand the contributions of this model. Numbers of administrators are succumbing to pressuring their staffs to set a goal of increasing testing scores. Yet, many note that kids may do best by going about the business of learning without being taught to the test, as Isaacson discovered when her entire school moved into constructivist teaching (Isaacson 2004) (see chapters 11 and 12). Benjamin (1989), in a prescient article, predicted this outcome as we began to swim into the testing movement.

THE NEXT COMPONENTS OF STRUCTURE:
HIERARCHY AND AUTHORITY

Hierarchy

When we create our organizations, we inevitably create positions. Almost inevitably, we place some positions above others in terms of having more power, authority, prestige, respect. In other words, we create a hierarchy of positions, some having more worth—and more power—than others. One reason for this is that organizations may work better in certain respects if the concept of division of labor is used. Even in the family, we use that idea. For example, in a traditional family, the wife may do the cooking, but may expect the husband to take out the garbage and to barbeque on the grill outdoors. In a more contemporary family, division of labor may not be as pronounced, and in some cases, roles may reverse, with husbands staying home to care for kids.

In more formal organizations, the Director of Medicine in a hospital has more authority and prestige than nurses or admitting clerks. Superintendents of schools have more authority than do bus drivers, meaning that superintendents can make decisions that generally will stick over a considerably wider area than the driver. Boards of Education have greater authority than even superintendents, since in most states they hire that person, and generally are expected to establish policies that superintendents are expected to carry out. In short, as Koren and Logaj (2009, 5) pointed out, "Permanent, unequal relations exist."

Authority

While the concept of hierarchy is pretty clear, that of *authority* is murkier, since a number of ways can be developed to look at it. Much of Western thinking has been affected by our several thousands of years of belief that authority is top-down. That is, we thought that authority came down from God to the king and then down to princes and down the line until we reached serfs who almost literally had no authority to order anyone about (except wives and kids, if they had them).

Barnard (1938) changed that notion forever when he laid out four conditions for a subordinate to *accept* the authority of a person's order.

1. The first condition is that subordinates must be able to understand the communication.
2. The second condition for accepting a directive is the person must feel that it conforms to the purposes of the organization.
3. The third condition is that the individual must believe that the order fits in with his or her own personal value system.
4. The fourth condition is that the person must be able to carry it out mentally and physically.

Let's see how this formulation plays out.

The first point is clear, since if we do not understand or perceive what the communication is all about, we cannot follow it. The second gets into the head of the subordinate. If the subordinate perceives or believes that the communication is counter to the purposes of the organization, we get a good deal of conflict, and probably fear. It's not easy to question a superior about a directive to do something without paying a penalty, which could include losing a job. All of a sudden, we have a more complex situation on our hands with Barnard's second point. The example of the My Lai massacre in Vietnam comes readily to mind. Did the troops at My Lai believe it was within the purposes of the American army to shoot unarmed old men, women, and children?

The third point Barnard makes is also tricky. A cousin of mine asked a number of his fellow soldiers during one of our wars if they could shoot someone. A goodly number of them indicated that it would be very hard to do—and the research bore this finding out. The role of the whistle-blower fits this point very well. We have had several cases of whistle-blowers emerging in major scandals, such as Enron, the case of the FBI missing vital information that field agents e-mailed regarding 9/11, and so forth. We even have legislation nationally that whistle-blowers are not to be attacked, although this does not seem to deter some.

The last point made by Barnard is self-evident. When we lived on the side of a hill in Nashville, Tennessee, if I had asked my then nine-year-old son to mow the lawn, he simply could not do it. It was difficult enough for an adult.

Now, let's see what Barnard has done with this formulation. First of all, Barnard has converted our linear thinking about authority into concentrating about *communicating*. Note that he focuses on the *subordinate accepting a communication*. Barnard has changed our way of thinking about authority as something absolute and handed down from above—into perceiving authority as a communication from a superior to a subordinate that is accepted! Essentially, we are dealing with *the process of communication* with this formulation, a major—no, a fundamental change in our thinking.

Authority as Communication?

Reflective Question

1. Is communication really the basis of authority?
2. Is this an example of a paradigm shift?

If Barnard is right, we are into a totally different ball game. Authority is now in the realm of *perception of communication*. In short, if I do not *accept* your communication, do you have authority? This comprises a 180-degree turnaround in thinking from viewing authority as coming from above, the king, to perceiving it as being *accepted by subordinates*.

A teacher/friend of mine became so fed up with a nit-picking chairman in her high school, that, much to his astonishment, she told him she wouldn't accept his authority anymore. And she didn't. This shoved him into quite a quandary, since I was the superintendent, and she was perceived, correctly, as a family friend. Eventually, he began to mend his ways since other faculty began to challenge his pickiness and excessive need for control, and he began to realize that his authority was slipping away.

ANOTHER UNIVERSAL
STRUCTURAL ELEMENT: SOCIAL SYSTEMS

But, First, Why Deal With Social Systems?

Cliques Are Social Systems

Reflective Questions

1. What do you think and feel when you hear the word "clique"?
2. Write five words about cliques on a separate piece of paper.
3. Are most negative? Why?

Generally—we react adversely. We believe that cliques exclude us, that they're formed of people who do not want to let us into "their" group, their territory. Actually, Webster's (Mish 1988) dictionary supports this, calling it "a narrow exclusive circle or group of persons; especially one held together by common interests, views, or purposes."

But is this valid, or just a result of years of being uncomfortable in our assumed notion that the clique may not let us in? Or is it that we think that members of cliques are not our kind of people with whom we would want to hang around, as Groucho Marx famously noted?

Whatever it is, cliques seem to have developed fairly negative reactions. They almost come across as the term "gang." If we switch terms and use the words *"social system"* instead, which is what social scientists such as sociologists call small groups in organizations, we suddenly have a tool to look at *the fundamental, the basic unit* of any organization. We are able to drop our less-than-positive-images and attitudes simply by changing the term. (This may become a technique to use as we think about how to improve our functioning in our daily professional behavior and practice.)

Social systems are the basic units of all groups, of all organizations. That is, organizations are composed of a whole series of small groups of people who hang together. What I'm saying is that the social system is the fundamental unit of structure in all organizations (Barnard 1938; Parsons and Shills 1951; Lammers 1987; Reed and Hughes 1992; Bausch 2001).

As a matter of fact, we are quite astute in watching who associates with whom in our organizations. We do this by watching who has lunch with whom, who talks with whom, who seems to want to work with each other, body language—and, we note it carefully.

The Family Is a Social System

Reflective Questions

1. Does the idea of social systems apply to families?
2. Which kids seem to like to work together (if you have more than a solo kid)?
3. Who sides with whom in arguments? Who is the favorite of each parent?
4. Who wants to go with whom when we do things together?

We have a lot of blended families. How careful are newish parents to treat everyone fairly? Is there a Cinderella? If so, what is the unspoken, the hidden curriculum in this family? Everyone can be damaged because the unspoken message is that it's OK to discriminate in this family, it's OK to pick on someone. Attitudes give clear messages. Kids will bring this hidden curriculum into their schools. So will teachers and administrators who come from families with these hidden beliefs.

Social Systems in Our Organizations

The same applies to all our organizations, such as faculty meetings, committees, work groups, etc. The astute principal will know quickly which people will want to work together on a project, just as the sensitive teacher will be able to predict which kids will want to work together—and who absolutely should not. (If you're going for a higher degree, make absolutely—no—positively certain that the people you ask to work on your committee like and respect each other—or your committee meetings will resemble a war with the members fighting each other while you watch helplessly, and you may become a casualty; a truly unpleasant outcome—for you!)

We must be sensitive to alliances people make with each other to work effectively, or we really will be operating blindly. If we cannot figure out those alliances—who likes and dislikes each other, who trusts and distrusts each other—we'll produce unneeded conflict. Key tasks either will not get done, or will sop up too much of our social capital (which is never unlimited). So picking up on who wants to work with whom, and who doesn't trust whom, is absolutely essential to being effective.

We've pretty well clarified how to recognize a social system when we meet one. Simply put, a social system is any two or more people interacting meaningfully (Getzels and Guba 1957). We are startled when we start to figure out how many social systems a group of only five people generates. Ten dyads (read, two's), six triads (read, three's), five social systems of four people, and the five itself is a social system. This totals twenty-two different social systems. Just trying to calculate the number of social systems in a small faculty of twenty or twenty-five people boggles the mind.

But, we are pretty astute. We usually can figure out key social systems or reference groups in a faculty, and know which person to approach to get different things done. Social systems also function to protect the individual from the organization.

UNIVERSAL ELEMENTS: NORMS (READ, CUSTOMS) AND DEVELOPING A POSITIVE CULTURE

As people in their social systems work and associate together, they develop expectations of each other's behavior. My kids would not start eating at Thanksgiving until their grandmother stopped caroming around the kitchen and sat down to eat. She, to give her credit, respected their custom, and would sit down to start off the meal.

We generally are quite unaware that we develop so many norms in our daily and professional lives. We were in a Dairy Queen, a family restaurant, when an older adolescent started using foul language (there were young children there). One of our friends told him in no uncertain terms that it was bad form to curse in front of the youngsters. The adolescent stopped violating the norms.

Note that behavior can be both acceptable and unacceptable simultaneously. His language might have been OK for his peers, but not for a family. And now we can see that patterns of norms become part of the culture of any society and group. In short, as we interact, we develop patterns of shared, learned behavior that we use in connection with living with others, a culture (Linton 1955). Everyone in a culture learns these patterns of shared expectations, which we pass on to youngsters. We generally do not have to tell six-year-olds not to bite other kids. They learn that early on. We all learn commonly expected and accepted ideas, values, attitudes, and habits as we grow up in a society and a culture.

It is only when we experience another culture that we become aware of our own cultural norms, as, for example, when my son and I went to an Ethiopian restaurant in Washington, D.C. First of all, tables were even lower than knee height sitting down, so you have to lean forward to eat. Then, since utensils are not cultural artifacts in that country, you have to tear off a piece of soft bread and pick up the food to eat it; however, they had napkins to wipe our fingers.

Reflective Question

Can you think of any examples of cultural differences in our country, such as food, language, buying habits, or regional differences, that you have come across?

- For example, Americans have breakfast foods, while some cultures do not, eating the same foods for all three or five meals. How about clambakes in New England, and the focus on corn dishes in the Midwest? The South has grits on which northerners often put maple syrup, to the dismay of waitresses.
- On returning from a trek in Nepal, our son listed "the top fifteen differences one notices on returning to the United States from Nepal and India." Among them are:
- White, peaked mountains, glacial lakes, five hundred seasonal foot waterfalls, and yak trains generally not considered pedestrian, commonplace sights.
- Relatively few cows hanging around in the middle of the road, grazing in one's neighborhood, around major tourist destinations, roaming through bus and train stations, waiting next to you on the train platform . . . heck, everywhere. . . .
- Beasts of burden, such as buffalo, oxen, and camels are considered fairly uncommon modes of transporting freight along the streets of most major American cities.

Developing Subcultures and Climates

All we have to do to pick up on *subcultures* is to head to different parts of our country. I once asked a native-born Southern friend of mine if his mother, who was preparing dinner, was making Southern fried chicken. He looked stunned, and really considered it bordering on being idiotic, but was polite (somewhat). He asked me what other fried chicken was there. Two friends seriously considered moving to Florida, but gave it up after realizing that the clambakes they loved in Connecticut would then belong to a former life.

Organizations, too, develop subcultures. Compare and contrast the subculture of an elementary school with that of a bank. Typically, banks present a relatively formal front to us customers, whereas the people in an elementary school are usually friendly and like the little people who bop around very seriously. Often, such schools are pretty informal—and very busy.

Owens (1988, 165) notes,

> . . . culture refers to the behavioral norms, assumptions, and beliefs of an organization, whereas *climate* refers to perceptions of persons in the organization that reflect those norms, assumptions, and beliefs.

As a consequence, one can assess the climate of any school with several instruments (Halpin and Croft 1963), including the *Organizational Climate Index* (Steinhoff 1965). Within organizations, parts may develop their own subculture and climate. Kindergarten teachers, for example, may have tons of stuff all over the place, while upper grades may not have as many manipulatives in every nook and cranny. Kindergarten kiddies usually have a milk-and-cookies break at mid-morning, naps in the afternoon, but not so in the fifth grade. Few banks have a cookies-and-milk mid-morning break and fewer have afternoon naps. Kindergarten kids usually have a recess, a dying practice for the upper grades in many schools today.

Reflective Questions

1. What different subcultures have developed in your school?
2. District, elementary schools?
3. How did they come about?

Can the Principal (and Teacher) Create a Positive Subculture and Climate? If So, How?

It's a key—and vital—question to ask, what is the role of the principal in creating a subculture? For most of us, this may be a somewhat startling question, but it gets to the heart of being an effective leader. Some leaders (and teachers, who are, of course, leaders in their classrooms and in other settings) take the role of the hapless Charlie Brown, standing around and being a passive observer as the norms and subcultures form. (Actually, Charlie helps them form, as Lucy and others observe sarcastically.)

Others may recognize that their role is to be more assertive. But we have to be clear that norms and subcultures are created in all groups as we interact with each other. Just because we do not recognize that they are forming does not mean that they are not coalescing around us. The big problem is that many of us usually are quite unaware as they develop around us, until they may hit us like a two-by-four.

This is certainly true in families, in classes, in schools, in the military, in stores. Whenever you have organizations, a subculture is created. Unfortunately, most of us really do not focus on this process, often until we belatedly recognize that some behavior patterns we do not like have mushroomed and slammed into our lives.

The leader, then, has to be very aware not only of the developing culture, but also the norms he or she wants to build. What would you like your school, or class, or school district to look like?

- People generally happy and supportive, developing trust for each other
- People being creative
- Taking risks to do good work
- Working cooperatively and supporting each other
- All people liking each other (or at least able to work with each other) and kids
- Being able to deal with inevitable conflict
- Using difference of opinions and conflict to improve things (how do we grow without conflict?)
- People working really hard, but smartly

Reflective Questions

1. What other behaviors would you like to see in your schools?
2. And if these become some of your goals, what can you do to pull them off?

A good deal of the rest of this book will deal with these questions—and more, for example, dealing with what a reflective principal does—and how does he or she behave in the complex world called school these days to make the school a productive, enriching place.

SUMMARY

In this part, we dealt with organizations, which we noted are man-made entities. We construct them, so that sociologists consider them as *socially constructed, shared realities.* We focused primarily on how organizations develop *structure* in their need to continue their viability. We generalized that organizations create *positions and roles* as the building blocks, the structure, of their existence. We noted that roles are expressed by role expectations, which can differ a great deal, so that our perceptions of a number of different interpretations can direct how we perform our roles.

Thus, we can generate a good deal of conflict as our role expectations develop. We found that we can have *conflicting expectations* for acting out one role, and that different reference groups often have divergent expectations regarding how our roles should be played out. Even within reference groups or social systems, role expectations may conflict. We suggested that Getzels' and Guba's model helped clarify sources of role conflict.

We also dug into two other components of structure, *hierarchy and authority*. We discovered the depth of Barnard's contribution to understanding authority with his formulation that for it to be accepted, four conditions were necessary. Thus, our contemporary grasp of authority presently is that it rests on *communication*—and its *acceptance by subordinates*, not on its delegation from higher levels.

Last, we focused on another key component of structure, the social system, which leads to the norms (read, customs) created by people interacting in social systems and organizations and resulting subcultures and climates that emerge. We noted that the social system is a key idea in understanding how organizations work.

Not only are families social systems, but also subgroups, which are social systems that inevitably form in all organizations, including friendship and work groups. Inevitably, we develop customs or norms in all our social systems, which develop into patterns, which become the subculture of the organization. Furthermore, we noted that we can create positive supportive subcultures if we become aware of the processes that generate subcultures. We will point to those processes as part of our case studies.

IMPORTANT TERMS

Authority—develops when subordinates accept communications as coming from a source vested with the *right* to make decisions

Climate—perceptions of people in an organization that reflect its norms, assumptions, beliefs

Culture—shared, learned behavior, assumptions, and beliefs that people in a society develop in connection with social living

Custom—a practice or behavior people in a group normally do (e.g., driving on the right)

Hierarchy—the structure of an organization; its levels

Idiographic dimension—the individual's personality and needs, need dispositions

Nomothetic dimension—roles and role expectations developed in an organization

Norm—a custom or practice of a group of people or culture

Organization—a formal body that has been organized or made into an organized whole

Position—various jobs or statuses in an organization, such as student, teacher, principal

Reference group—a group people regard as prestigious

Role—the dynamic enactment of a position; a series of expectations defining the role

Role conflict—occurs when expectations for a role are perceived to differ

Role expectations—various expectations different reference groups develop for a role

Social system—any two or more people in a meaningful relationship

Structure—the internal organization of an organization

Subculture—the mini-culture that people in parts of a culture develop, such as in an organization

4

Hidden Eddies That Can Drive
Us Off Course

Metaphors and Images of Organizations That Often Dominate Our Thinking—and a Curriculum-Steering Task Force That *Generates Controlled Change as a Routine*

> The behavior of an organization often can be predicted by assuming it is controlled by a cabal of its enemies.
>
> —Robert Conquest's Law

SO, WHAT DO WE MEAN BY METAPHORS AND IMAGES OF ORGANIZATIONS (READ, SCHOOLS)?

Reflective Questions

1. Do you want to be able to describe, analyze, and predict what your leaders and leaders in other organizations are going to do? (That would be some advantage!)
2. OK, then the first step to take is: have you ever wondered why we think about organizations the way we do?
3. But—can we also become prisoners of our beliefs, of our metaphors?

Whenever we use language to describe anything, we use symbols. Kids tend to simplify symbols such as noting that a shovel is to dig with, a chair is to sit on. When we talk about organizations, we also think about and describe them in symbols, but we tend to be more abstract, often using *metaphors*, *images*, or *symbols* to get at their nature and function. Metaphors, in short, are "ways of thinking, ways of seeing" (Morgan 1997).

In this chapter we'll look at various metaphors, symbols, and ways of thinking people use to describe and to analyze organizations, which often lead to influencing our behavior—sometimes even without our being aware of it.

Surprised?

Perhaps, if we also can predict how each of the specific metaphors analyzed here influences how we behave, we may be able to decide which metaphor(s) to adopt to make our personal and professional lives in our organizations more productive and satisfying. In other words, we can construct metaphors as models that can be highly useful by predicting the consequences of using each metaphor on how we act.

These metaphors, as Morgan (1997) and others portray them, picture our organizations as:

- A machine
- An organism
- A political arena or system—(in short, sometimes a battlefield)
- A culture
- A self-learning system or a learning organization
- Involved in change (wherein we present a Curriculum-Steering Committee structure *to generate change as a routine* through the school or system).
- A family
- A psychic prison, or an instrument of domination (such as a bad marriage)
- A social sorting mechanism
- A refuge

THE WORLD (PARTICULARLY SCHOOLS) AS A MACHINE, SPECIFICALLY, AS A CLOCK

In Monty Python's (1983) film, *The Meaning of Life*, we see rows of accountants in their black suits and white shirts in a London (or is it Atlanta?) office decked out like a galley, slavishly pulling their calculator's handles (symbolically oars) mindlessly in unison. What is the message?

Why did the engineers in General Electric's Hawthorne plant in Cicero, Illinois, think that if they increased the comforts for the six wire relay workers (a longer lunch hour, a break in the morning, brighter lights), they would produce more? Indeed, that is exactly what happened when the engineers improved each of the working conditions. The workers produced more at each positive change. No surprise. "So far, so good," thought the engineers.

Then, they slowly took away each of the "goodies" (reduced the lunch hour)—production increased. They eliminated the break—production increased. They dimmed the lighting so that the room resembled a bright, moonlit night, but production still increased. Why didn't the relay workers produce less, as expected by the engineers? Much to the engineers' amazement, the workers increased production each time a "goodie" was removed, no matter what the engineers did to reduce motivation.

So, what was lurking behind the thinking, the assumptions, the beliefs, of the engineers? They had bought into the current notion that the world was a gigantic machine, specifically, a clock (remember, we are talking about the 1920s)—and people were expected to operate mechanically—as clocks do. That was the current world view in the early twentieth century—for some, it still is (as we shall see).

In short, it was the current metaphor (image), or way we think of the world that drove their, and our, behavior. The engineers thought that the wire relay workers were machines—and if they were rewarded, they would jump (like Pavlov's dogs salivating at the ringing of the bell [except that some of his dogs did not salivate—they became angry!]), and would produce more. Similarly, if the rewards, the goodies, were reduced, they would in turn reduce their effort; a stimulus reflex theory, so to speak.

Wrong.

The women workers were (and are) not machines. Neither were Monty Python's accountants.

But why did the engineers think this way? In the early twentieth century, people bought into the notion that the world was a gigantic machine, like a clock—and they also applied this metaphor to what ran people (who hardly function like machines).

Interestingly, that does not deter many organizations from implementing machine-like systems, that is, bureaucracies, to improve production—even to this day. We need only look as far as most fast-food organizations to see that they've organized production lines that treat workers as machines, as do insurance companies who count the number of cases clerks work on to decide whether to fire them on Friday—or, not. Or, Wal-Mart.

While Max Weber (1946) pulled all the elements of bureaucracy together into a system, Frederick Taylor (1911), who founded the Scientific Management theory of leadership (highly dictatorial) and human motivation, provided concrete recommendations to make organizations work like machines. Taylor treated the workers at the bottom of the organizational hierarchy as machines by simplifying jobs so workers were:

- easy to standardize
- easy to replace
- easy to train

- easy to supervise
- cheap

Now, do you see why I mentioned the fast-food industry's use of the teenagers of America as mainstay employees? They're cheap, easy to replace, the systems standardize the kids, they're easy to supervise (nineteen-year-old supervisors yell at the younger kids), the computers have pictures so poor readers can punch them.

Taylor invented the notion of paying people by piecework—so Wal-Mart decides whether to keep people by looking at how many items they scan in an hour. How's that for standardizing?

Reflective Question

Have we teachers and principals been Taylorized?

The federal No Child Left Behind law (NCLB) and state knockoffs threaten schools and teachers who do not meet politically inflated goals (all students in this Lake Wobegon Eden will read on grade level by 2012) with replacement. (Of course, if the states could figure out how to deal with the pervasive poverty and its educational consequences generated by the American productive system, they would come in and help out.)

So, a century after Taylor developed his system, amazingly, it is in wide use in our society, organizations—and in the schools. That's because the elites who run the nation's political system firmly believe that if they pressure educators enough, we'll jump and produce more—just like machines. And, sure enough, some of us do.

But, are we machines?

We already have substitute credentialing programs that permit untrained people to teach and even to become administrators. So, we are being treated as easy to standardize, easy to replace, very easy to train (anyone can apply who has any degree [or maybe, even not]), easy to supervise, and very cheap.

Builds lots of resentment, doesn't it? Note lots of anger at NCLB (Hunt, Benjamin, and Shapiro 2004; Shapiro and Thompson 2009).

What Can We Do to Subvert This Process?

If we choose to treat organizations as mechanical devices, we destroy treating people as individuals. People become widgets to manipulate for our gain. Treating the organization (read, school) as a machine generates discontent and major problems for kids, teachers, and leaders—and, essentially, is a fallacy. Our schools are hardly machines. Nor are we. We have to change the metaphor, or we'll screw up since beliefs and metaphors drive behavior.

So, the following provide some metaphors to choose among.

THE SCHOOL AS AN ORGANISM

Reflective Question

What on earth does this mean? And, how can I/we pull this off?

The school as an organism seems to be the exact opposite of schools as machines, where the focus is on each part. Here the focus is on the whole, the gestalt, much like treating the forest as an ecosystem. Well, the school itself is a system set within a host of other systems (school district, neighborhood, local community, etc.). And within the school are other systems such as the governance or management subsystem, the psychosocial, technology, structural, and environmental subsystems (Luciano 1979). So, viewing schools as a system with subsystems gives us a way to treat schools quite differently than as machines.

But, as with the machine as a valid descriptor and analyzer of schools, this metaphor also misleads. The metaphor of an organism seems to imply a living entity, and while organizations and schools seem to survive (but not necessarily thrive) a long time generally, they are not literally living things. They are human constructs, but not quite organisms. Still, treating the school as a whole, as an organism, is useful in *constructing* our behavior because it points out to us that the school is like a pond. One act can cause ripples and even waves all over the place.

As discussed further in the section on culture, Dr. Leanna Isaacson, the principal cited in chapters 11 and 12, pulled this off by having each team celebrate a Wonderful Wednesday program monthly. They also used the Seattle Fish Market philosophy of having fun on the job, as well as having other celebrations and parties, treating their school as a whole, as an organism. And did it change the culture of the schools!

ORGANIZATIONS (READ, SCHOOLS) AS POLITICAL ARENAS OR SYSTEMS—IN SHORT, BATTLEFIELDS

In a class last night, a teacher commented that her principal assigned top-level students (5s) to her favorite teachers, 4s to less favorites, and 1s to people she didn't like at all. And her co-teachers warned her that if she complained, the principal would make her life a living hell. The principal's buddies of twenty years got all the "goodies."

So, a new teacher found out that some people had more power, more influence than she did. Of course, one of the outcomes was a discussion on why the district permitted the principal to practice such poor grouping procedures despite major research findings over the last century. One conclusion emerged that in a very large district, principals can hide under the radar and, therefore, can get away with a lot, particularly if they accumulate a lot of influence and power themselves.

Many of us see organizations as arenas in which people and factions struggle to dominate and to control each other, as the principal described above clearly does. Indeed, this sometimes is valid where organizations are used as vehicles for individuals and factions to maneuver for power and control for things that some define as "goodies."

And what are goodies for some of us?

- Power
- Influence
- Control
- Love
- Respect

Reflective Question

What else would you add to this?

Often, we believe that power, control, authority, are finite, limited. If you have power, it means that I can have less. Is this belief valid?

Political systems essentially provide arenas for the distribution, gain, loss, and exercise of power, authority, and influence—that is, organizational goodies. The preceding chapter 3 referred to Chester Barnard's (1938) rethinking of authority from coming down from the powers above to the *subordinate accepting* it because it comes from a person who has *the right* to exercise authority. Thus, the direction or order to do something has to meet the four conditions Barnard cites. That is:

- the person understands the communication,
- it meets the person's perceptions that it does not conflict with the person's own value system,
- it does not conflict with the person's perception of the values of the organization,
- and the person can actually do what is expected in the order.

According to Barnard, the teacher has to *accept* the communication based on these four conditions, not because the principal has a god-given right to rule as conferred upon her by the superintendent and board of education. Some difference!

Political systems also may provide processes to deal with the conflict and resentments that inevitably arise as people organize and work with each other in close contact. For example, when businesses and schools develop a contract with those who work there, it usually stipulates how conflicts may be treated. Grievance procedures essentially provide a method to deal with and potentially to reduce conflict generated by the social systems within the organization.

However, a teachers' association or union usually organizes so that each unit (school, factory) has a union representative. I find myself quite often dealing with people who complain about this or that concern or issue they raise by suggesting that they contact their union rep to help resolve the problem. That is an institutionally designed vehicle to deal with organizational conflict (which is a pretty fancy way to say that it's a way to deal with differences of opinion—and to keep the organization going).

Another process to handle people's issues and concerns regarding conflict consists of running conflict resolution workshops, since many people do not like to confront conflict-laden situations and/or people. This is particularly true of elementary faculty. These workshops are often a major way to handle situations which may fester when people are loath to confront an aggressor, be it a peer teacher or a principal.

How Can We Subvert This Process?

Organizations pretty obviously are political systems, which can degenerate into battlefields. How can we make sure that power is distributed so that everyone has a stake in the school, and develop the appropriate buy-in necessary to develop productive schools and classes? It is not useful to set up systems where people feel ignored, powerless, and consequently become alienated. Systems have to be developed for all to feel they have a voice in decisions, such as making sure to involve new folks on all kinds of committees.

(See the section in this chapter on Organizations as Change and particularly the structure and process laid out for establishing and running a Curriculum-Steering Committee Structure. This serves as an internal structure that *generates change* through a school or a district with massive involvement *as a routine*. Strategies to increase inclusion and involvement are major keys to effective leadership.)

ORGANIZATIONS (SCHOOLS) AS CULTURE

Reflective Question

Do you know of any organization that does not generate a culture?

Families certainly do. So do kindergartens. The Marine Corps culture is somewhat different from that of a kindergarten. Elementary schools generate different cultures than high schools or colleges, and are quite different from that of your local garage repair shop, a culture being a series of practices and customs that people develop in connection with social living (Linton 1955). Cultures develop a shared language, symbols, beliefs, norms or customs, and mores that we dare not break (cannibalism, incest).

So, clearly, organizations do develop a culture. Now, the problem for us is to figure out how to pull off developing a culture that is satisfying and supportive for us professionals, that permits us to be productive at the same time.

OK, what are the elements of a culture in any organization? Norms, or customs, or everyday practices are major components. We can easily think of them when we have two or three kids in the back of our cars (and they are completely applicable in our classrooms).

- Listen to others politely
- Do not interrupt
- Never attack others verbally or physically
- Share things like candy

Actually, very strongly held norms are mores, which we learn early on and consist of behavior that is absolutely unacceptable, such as biting someone, or not wearing completely unacceptable clothes to school (a bathing suit). Can you think of other examples?

Reflective Questions

1. What about norms for our schools and districts?
2. Can we see organizations from a different perspective?

OK, to state it straight out: organizations are actually created (we create them), *socially constructed, and shared realities* (organizations involve more than one person, so to be in one means we are in a shared setting—and they sure are shared).

What about opportunities to serve on committees that make major decisions, such as textbook selection or committees to recommend persons for leadership positions. (I had high school students serve on principal selection committees [they usually could detect phonies faster than we professionals could.])

Dr. Isaacson, principal of a constructivist school in Orlando, Florida, developed monthly Wonderful Wednesdays, where every team took responsibility for a theme for the faculty to have fun around. These Wednesdays became high points of each month, opportunities for creativity for each team.

They also adapted the FISH philosophy. The idea of having fun came from the Seattle Fish Market, where employees changed a messy, smelly job into one where they became creative, adding variety and fun to their jobs (for example, by throwing fish to each other). The strategies used in changing her school from a large, almost one-thousand-student elementary school to a highly decentralized and effective model are described and analyzed in chapters 11 and 12.

As a consequence, we discovered a major *affect* factor by the third year of work with the faculty, that of people feeling "I love my family." As a piece of this, the school developed a norm that they would not let new teachers shift for themselves and possibly fail, and essentially created Professional Learning Communities (PLCs) (Clauset 2008) where teachers could get ideas, support, and suggestions from peers.

New teachers were given a couple of periods every two weeks to work with mentors to learn new techniques, approaches, and methods of reaching hard-to-reach kids, etc. Teacher retention skyrocketed—no one wanted to leave. Recruitment became a nonissue, since people loved being there, even though they had to drive long distances. The school itself became a PLC.

What Can We Do to Pull This Off?

If we're clever enough to build a better mousetrap (read, school culture), problems can be finessed, avoided—and life can become a lot easier for all of us. So, if schools *are created, socially constructed, shared realities (we create them*—and then they can create us), we can use our creativity to make them places where we like and want to be, as Dr. Isaacson did in her school. Note that the faculty were determined to help new teachers grow and to help keep them in education.

SCHOOLS AS SELF-LEARNING SYSTEMS— OR, A LEARNING ORGANIZATION

As usual, a metaphor can sharpen or can blur reality. This does the latter.

The people in the school or business can set up internal structures to work on improving their practices, but the organization can hardly be considered as a learning system. That's an anthropomorphism—that is assigning human characteristics to objects or animals. It's the *people* who learn—and the culture within the organization that accepts or rejects change, that is open to new realties or is closed to them. We just discussed the notion that individuals and groups (social systems) develop shared, social realities (organizations), which can prosper or can go to pieces. The curriculum-steering structure is probably the closest thing to generating perpetual controlled change as I've come across to pulling this off, as indicated in the reflective question below.

Reflective Question

Can we set up an internal structure or system whereby change can be *generated as a routine process?*

See the very next section, Schools as Involved in Change, for an ingenious process and structure that does exactly that.

How to Pull This Off?

Read this next section.

SCHOOLS AS INVOLVED IN CHANGE: (WHEREIN WE PRESENT A CURRICULUM-STEERING COMMITTEE STRUCTURE TO GENERATE CHANGE THROUGH THE SCHOOL OR SYSTEM AS A ROUTINE)

Western organizations, clearly, are experiencing enormous changes. For example, General Motors, once the gold star of auto makers, has gone from over half the market to well under 25 percent, closing plants and cutting jobs in the process.

How about schools?

When I teach a course called Change and Change Strategies, I ask people in groups to list ten major changes in society in the past twenty-five years, and then follow that up with an exercise asking about ten major changes in education in the same time period. We can generate thirty in just a few minutes: testing, technology, NCLB, virtual learning, home schooling, vouchers, charter schools, etc., etc.

Reflective Questions

1. But how do we *generate controlled change?*
2. And how do we generate change through any school system *as a routine*, so that the change is expected as part of the everyday operation of the school and of the leadership?

As an assistant superintendent and superintendent, I was involved in establishing just such a system, a *Curriculum-Steering Task Force or Committee*, whose job was to stimulate, analyze, and evaluate curriculum proposals and then recommend them for adoption.

Pretty neat? And, it worked!

Here's how. Of course, members of the Curriculum-Steering Committee (Shapiro 2003) were key administrators, the leadership and troops of the Union, and a Board member. In one district where trust was an issue, student and community representatives were heavily included. Took a bit of time, but was worth it.

The structure and process follow:

CURRICULUM COMMITTEE STRUCTURE AND RULES

I. Purpose
   A. The purpose of the *area committee* is to review and to recommend to the Steering Committee all changes in curriculum related to their area. The stimulus for change comes from teachers' work groups. The area committee will concern itself with contact and curriculum concepts.
   B. The purpose of the Steering Committee is similar to that of the area committee but on a much broader basis. The Steering Committee will review and recommend to the upper administration and Board of Education all changes in curriculum. The members of the committee cannot be expert in all curricular areas; however, some group must be responsible for the ever changing curricular process. The main judgment will be in terms of a priority which is best for the total school district.

II. Structure
   A. A committee to be established for each of the major curriculum areas, these to be known as area committees (see attached diagram):
      1. Humanities, including Social Studies, English-Language Arts, Fine Arts (music, art, drama)
      2. Mathematics—Science
      3. Applied Arts, including Business, Home Economics, Industrial Arts, Vocational courses, Physical Education, Health and Safety
      4. Special Areas, including Outdoor Education, Slow Learner and Special Education, Accelerated Learner, Evaluation, Preschool Education, Educational Media, Extracurricular Performance Activities (athletics, drama, speech, etc.)

      Each area committee may select work groups for carrying out specific tasks—responsible to the parent committee. The entire staff will be considered a committee of the whole to be drawn upon as needed by the individual area committees and subcommittees.
   B. Each area committee to be composed of three teachers from elementary, middle, and high schools (totaling nine teachers) plus

one principal and the assistant superintendent for instruction. (The Applied Arts Committee shall be composed of four teachers plus one principal and the assistant superintendent for instruction.)

This structure may be altered only in rare instances to conform to what is needed at a particular time.

C. Membership on each area committee to be by preference, final selection to be made by the assistant superintendent and chairman of each respective committee (plus one member selected by both), with the advice of the principals and the approval of the superintendent. Membership of the Curriculum-Steering Committee to be composed of:

(5) Two representatives appointed by DeKalb Classroom Teachers' Association (DCTA) President, and three teachers to be selected at large (one elementary, one middle, one high school) by the Assistant Superintendent for Instruction, one principal, and DCTA President.

(4) Chairmen (teachers only)

(3) Principals

(1) Director of Research

(1) Assistant Superintendent of Instruction

(1) Assistant Superintendent for Pupil Personnel

(1) Superintendent (Ex-Officio)

D. Principals to choose the committee they will work on according to interest and/or competency. They are not eligible to serve as chairman or may not be elected recorder but are requested to serve on work committees.

E. Chairman from previous school year to act as chairman pro tem until new permanent chairman for the year has been elected. If not chairman, present principal to serve as chairman pro tem until permanent chairman is elected.

F. Chairman to work with the principals on the respective committees and communicate with the total committee through the principals, who will work directly with the assistant superintendent and through the assistant superintendent's office. Minutes will be typed by building secretaries.

G. The agenda, minutes, and proposals for each area committee are to be approved by the chairman and sent in final form to the assistant superintendent for curriculum and instruction's office where they will be duplicated and distributed to all principals and committee members, DCTA building representatives, representatives of the special services council, the assistant superintendent, superintendent, and Board of Education.

H. Meetings to be held once a month from 3:45 to 5:00 p.m. on a regular school day with overall Steering Committee meetings once a month on the first Tuesday, at 3:45 p.m. The agenda and minutes of the Steering Committee and all proposals to be considered by them shall be sent to all committee chairman and principals, DCTA building representatives, representative of the special services council, the assistant superintendent, superintendent, and Board of Education.

I. Prior to the establishment of work groups, the prospective proposal must be submitted to the area committee and the assistant superintendent for instruction.

III. Rules

A. The only matters to be considered by the Steering Committees are those that are associated with curriculum, as defined by IIA.

B. All members of the Steering Committee are voting members.

C. Two-thirds of the members of the Steering Committee shall constitute a quorum.

D. Recommendation shall be approved by the Steering Committee when they receive a positive vote by two-thirds of the membership of the committee. The record of the vote on a particular recommendation shall not be recorded when it is approved and sent to the administration and Board of Education.

E. When a recommendation fails, it is returned to the recommending committee for reconsideration with any explanation necessary. It may be resubmitted.

F. Recommendations that are approved by the Steering Committee are submitted to the administration and Board of Education for action.

G. Recommendations received during the school year will be tentatively approved or rejected and returned to the recommending committees. Those that are tentatively approved will be collected through the year when they will be given priority ratings by members of the Steering Committee.

H. Any recommendations for changing curriculum offerings must be submitted through the area committee to the Steering Committee, prior to the Steering Committee's first meeting in April. All proposals shall have a first reading at a Steering Committee meeting and then may be approved at the next meeting.

I. Priority ratings of tentatively approved proposals will be made on the basis of a 1 (top rating); 2 (second priority); or 3 (low priority). Recommendations reported out of the Steering Committee will be placed in one of the three categories for action by the administration and Board of Education.

J. A final report shall be filed by each area committee incorporating all sub-committee and area committee work for the next year. This final report shall include:

(a) A summary of the year's work in all areas;

(b) Findings from the study and recommendations for improvement;

(c) Direction studies should take for the ensuing year.

The total report, which will include the rating of recommendations, will be made available to every school and area chairman. A short form report summarizing actions on recommendations and final reports will be made available to every staff member in the school district and to the Board of Education.

K. Recommendations not implemented shall be returned to the recommending committee for reconsideration and resubmission.

L. The following format shall be the standard for all recommendations submitted to the area and Steering Committees.

FORMAT TO BE USED FOR PREPARING AND SUBMITTING RECOMMENDATIONS FOR CURRICULUM IMPROVEMENT

1. Introduction—Rationale stating purpose, goals, and objective—stated behaviorally, if possible
2. Required materials, staff, other
   (a) Immediate
   (b) Long range
3. Justification for Recommendations
4. Cost implied by Recommendations
5. Method of Evaluation
6. Mode of Dissemination
7. Other

All statements to be dated. Fifteen copies of every recommendation shall be provided when the proposal is submitted.

SCHOOLS AS FAMILIES

My gifted wife, reading Morgan's (1997) list of metaphors, noted that he left out the family. So, here goes. Actually, Chester Barnard (1938), in changing the way we perceived organizations, rejected the notion that a corporation literally is its table of organization. He pointed out that it is the informal suborganizations, the social systems, that breathe life into the organization, are the underlying structure that makes the corporation go.

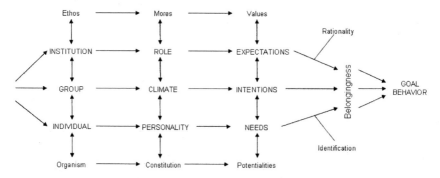

Figure 4.1. Social behavior and administrative process (Getzels and Guba, Winter, 1957)

These suborganizations are the social systems (any two or more people involved in meaningful interaction) that form the basis of the organization, be it a family, or a department, or a grade of small learning community. So, the school breaks down into small subunits, social systems, which can become close, intimate, friendship groups who socialize together, celebrate birthdays and the winter holidays, etc. In short, they may begin to feel and act like a family.

My wife's close cluster of friends from her community college meet regularly for lunch, and several of my colleagues and I and our wives have been meeting every other Sunday evening for more than two decades. We've become a highly supportive family.

But, the decentralization into SLCs and PLCs can accelerate this process. Isaacson's teachers (chapters 11 and 12) expressed the feeling that they loved their group and felt that they had created a family.

ORGANIZATIONS (SCHOOLS, FAMILIES) AS PSYCHIC PRISONS

Reflective Question

Have you, or someone you know, ever been divorced?

Do you, or they, feel that they were in a prison? Something they were caught in—and couldn't get out of?

When I teach classes involved in understanding organizations (obviously, that's most courses in leadership programs), I always ask that question—whether anyone has ever been divorced. The follow-up question is really the stopper. "Did you ever feel you were in a prison?"

People usually fall silent—and then, some nod.

Curriculum Steering Committee Structure: District

┌───┐
│ Curriculum Steering Committee   │
└───┘

(5)   2 representatives appointed by CTA President and 3 teachers to be

        selected at large (1 elementary, 1 middle school, 1 high school by Ass't Supt. for

        instruction, one Principal & CTA President

(4)   Chairman of Area Committees (all teachers)

(3)   Principals

(1)   Director of Research

(1)   Assistant Superintendent for instruction

(1)   Assistant Superintendent for Pupil Personnel

(1)   Superintendent (Ex-Official)

┌──────────────┐ ┌──────────────┐ ┌──────────────┐ ┌──────────────┐
│ Humanities   │ │ Special Areas│ │ Math-Science │ │ Humanities   │
│ Area Committee│ │ Area Committee│ │ Area Committee│ │ Area Committee│
└──────────────┘ └──────────────┘ └──────────────┘ └──────────────┘

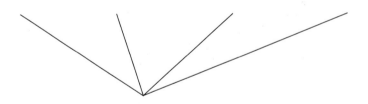

(9) teachers—(3 from each of :

    elementary, middle and high school)

    - (1) Principal and Assistant Supt. for Instruction

Work Groups ⟶ ⟵ Assistant Superintendent ⟶ ⟵ Work Groups

Figure 4.2.   A centralized curriculum structure

If someone feels comfortable discussing it, they describe themselves as locked in a prison from which they've despaired of escaping. This is especially true of abused spouses.

Families are organizations. Couples are organizations—as are schools.

Any organization can become a psychic prison. Even schools. How? Simple. Set up an arbitrary test. Insist that all kids pass it with an average score. Then fail large numbers of kids like Florida did (thirty-three thousand third graders the first year).

Voila! The school becomes a psychic prison since little kids cannot escape. Then, compound it by making sure that the kids take the test again the second time they remain third graders. If they flunk, keep them a third year in grade three, so that they're two years older than the other kids. Florida is doing this now, so expect the dropout rate to skyrocket when these kids become sixteen, are now in eighth grade—and drive to school.

Or organize the school on an ability basis. Be sure to set up a "dumb dumb" class. The kids will point out the "dumb dumbs." Humiliation is a given.

Reflective Questions

1. What other examples can we give?
2. How about a worse question? Can we become prisoners of our metaphors, our beliefs so we do not know any alternatives?

How about staying in a toxic relationship because we cannot imagine any other alternative? Or, some people even believe that they deserve the abuse.

How about administrators who believe that they must be authoritarian to get things done?

What about the United States' and the UK's fixation on testing as an accountability mechanism ("Leading for results") in comparison with Finland and Scandinavia's focus on ("Leading for learning") (Oldroyd 2003)? Our accountability movement is a top-down, coercive, Taylorian approach; but the Finland and Scandinavian approach is producing far better results. Yet our policy makers have become obsessed with the testing device as their tool of choice to force accountability on us.

Except that it does not seem to work.

And as a matter of fact, the accountability movement is thoroughly behaviorist. That is, behaviorism ignores how people think and develop meaning, only focusing on measurable behavior, not looking at the meanings people give to their and others' behavior (Koren and Shapiro 2009).

Reflective Question

Can you think of any other examples?

A SOCIAL SORTING MECHANISM

Reflective Question

What do we mean by this?

I asked my daughter, Alana, when she was a sophomore in high school, what the social structure of the school was. "Well," she replied, "there are the beautiful people who only talk to themselves. Then there are the preppies, then the jocks, then the geeks (like Bill Gates, who become the real successes), then several groups of kids who have become the 'rejectees' who hardly participate at all, the underclass of the school."

Brantlinger (1995), Kozol (1991), Howard (1989), and lots of people point to the social sorting nature of the school, where kids learn where their place in society is. Kids learn this readily. How can we spot this? Upper-middle-class students flock into band and orchestra, take advanced placement and honors courses, and get into the IB program and specialized academies (medical, performing arts), National Honor Society, etc. The vehicle for this is ability grouping and tracking (Oakes 1985; Shapiro, Benjamin, and Hunt 1995).

Reflective Question

What can we do to subvert this process?

What about generating a program of courses open to everyone? We did this in several schools, breaking year-long courses into minis or nine weeks, so they were quarter-semester courses, or semester-long courses. So you can have a host of history courses (*"The Atomic Age," "Myths and Realities about The Old West," "The Roaring 20s,"* a simulated *"Archaeological Dig"*).

Next, hook them up with Language Arts, so that you have a bunch of interdisciplinary humanities courses (*"The Civil War"* with books such as *Andersonville, Red Badge of Courage,* and *Gone with the Wind,* for example). Science can have a nine-weeker, such as *"The Fetal Pig,"* beloved by biologists worldwide.

In other words, build an *interest-based curriculum* so that no course or sequence has greater prestige. This approach totally finessed the upper-middle-class soccer moms who are so wedded to symbols of prestige for their kids.

SCHOOLS AS A REFUGE

Reflective Question

Seriously?

Certainly. Most of the time schools are safe from abusive families. Kids who are hungry (about 20 percent plus of our kids) can get breakfast and lunch. One young woman, who co-taught with me, eventually told me that she and her brother would scavenge for food in dumpsters after school, commenting that at least they ate breakfast and lunch during the week. She was not too fond of her father, calling him "that bastard."

We now have become aware of student homelessness and so some of us are alert to signs of that. My wife tells of a kid in high school who, unknown to the teachers and maybe most of the kids, was kicked out of his home. He came to school every day, and only at the end of the year did they find out that he was sleeping in one of the baseball field's dugouts, showering, and then coolly coming to school.

How did he perceive school? As a refuge.

In school, lots of kids get recognition and other rewards (Maslow's esteem level in his hierarchy of human needs). So, schools really can become refuges for kids. But can they for adults? When I work with schools, we almost always establish a *recognition system or committee* where *everyone* gets recognized with a photo plus comments on the accomplishment in a very public place. We even establish a special committee to do this. What does everyone mean? All adults and kids—all. People crowd around the area.

When I worked in the inner city of Chicago, we used to have sweaters, boots, shirts, and the like for kids who were freezing in the city's frigid winters. In some places, the fraternal clubs provided glasses.

SUMMARY

We took a brief look at some major metaphors or images we use to think about organizations, and specifically schools. In order, they were schools as machines and its opposite, gestalt-type organisms. Then, we explored the school as a battlefield or a political arena, next a culture, and then a self-learning system with a Curriculum-Steering Committee or Task Force. We then continued analyzing and evaluating schools as families and as psychic prisons, and last as social sorting mechanisms and as refuges.

We continually asked Reflective Questions, which we hope were on target and even discomforting—and suggested ways to subvert some of the negative consequences of some metaphors. We even laid out the Curriculum-Steering Committee's rules and norms as a way to make change a routine, thus avoiding the stress that sudden change generates in systems.

IMPORTANT TERMS

Anthropomorphic—assigning human characteristics to inanimate objects or animals

Culture—shared, learned behavior, assumptions, and beliefs that people in a society develop in connection with social living

Metaphor—ways of seeing, ways of thinking, a figure of speech in which a word or phrase literally denoting one kind of object or idea is used in place of another to suggest a likeness or analogy between them

More—very strongly held customs

Norms—customs, practices

5

Five Hidden Whirlpools (*Pulls, or Centers of Influence*) That the Five Parts of Organizations Inevitably Generate

When your knowledge changes, the universe changes.

We are what we know.

—James Burke, *The Day the Universe Changed*

I hate organizational asymmetries of privilege.

—Roy Weatherford, President, United Faculty of Florida

Reflective Question

This is another chapter where we can ask, do you want to be able to describe, analyze, and predict very accurately the behavior of your leaders and those in other organizations?

This model we're describing offers a powerful predictor and analyzer of both short and long-range behavior of those in leadership and in peonship positions—enabling each of us to predict pretty well how various parts of our organizations are going to behave, so we can try to control our own professional lives better.

So, read on.

In Section II, "How Organizations Work," is chapter 3, "How to Make Sure We Stay Afloat (How to Work with the Dynamics of the School, So We

Don't Screw Up Too Badly)—And How to Create a Healthy Subculture in the Process." In it we dealt with developing structure such as *positions,* then *roles* and *role expectations,* which can lead to *role conflict,* then *hierarchy* and *authority,* which Barnard argued was based on communications.

That chapter's section, "Universal Elements: Social Systems," zeroed in on social systems (read, groups) that form universal informal structures within the formal structure of the organization. We found that the formal and informal organizations inevitably develop a *culture* and numerous *subcultures,* and suggested that we can improve our lives in our schools by creating subcultures we want. Of course, we can only do that if we know what we're doing. (Incidentally, not knowing what we're doing can lead to our undoing.)

In the succeeding chapter, chapter 4, "Hidden Eddies That Can Drive Us Off Course: Metaphors and Images of Organizations. . . ," we dealt with images and metaphors of organizations that may drive our behavior of which we may or may not be aware.

This present chapter 5 digs away at key but often hidden patterns that inevitably occur, but that are generally so unobtrusive that they often slip by us, leaving most of us blissfully unaware of them. But do they impact us daily! Let's see as we unfold them.

These influences consist of *pulls* that various parts of organizations, that is, levels of social systems within organizations, inevitably develop that seem so irrational—until we grasp the dynamics of the pulls—and then they make clear sense, explaining all kinds of behavior that may puzzle and even exasperate us tremendously. This behavior may look dysfunctional, but isn't if you begin to understand how and why these pulls operate.

PREDICTING PULLS FOR POWER AND CONTROL FROM DIFFERENT PARTS OF ORGANIZATIONS

Reflective Question

Did you ever wish you'd written a particular book?

I have. It's *The Structuring of Organizations* by Henry Mintzberg (1979), in which he developed a logo delineating five different parts of the organization. See figure 5.1.

The first is the *Strategic Apex* (the lads and ladies in control, the Top Dogs, so to speak, the Central Office). The *Middle Line* consists of middle management (principals and her assistants, deans; in business and factories, managers and foremen). The *Operating Core* consists of us peons who do the work, teachers, aides, etc.

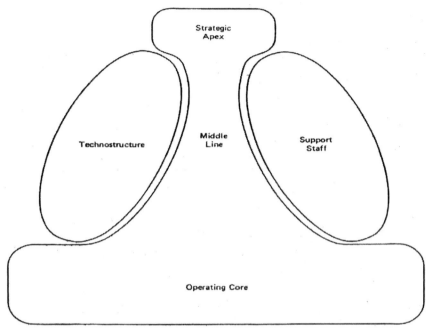

Figure 5.1. Mintzberg's Logo: Five Basic Components of Organizations

Source: Henry Mintzberg, *Structuring of Organizations,* 1st ed. © 1979, p. 20. Reprinted by permission of Pearson Education, Inc., Upper Saddle River, NJ.

Two more groups people the organization: the *Technostructure* consisting of technocrats, such as computer people and other analysts, and *Support Staff,* which include office, cafeteria, custodians. (You know, the people who make the organization work on a daily basis.)

My reason for pulling Mintzberg into this chapter is simple. He points to each social system as exerting *a different, and crucial, "pull"* on the organization because of its interests. See figure 5.2.

Predicting these pulls can make you seem like a genius—because you will be miles ahead of everyone in predicting the actions of each organization's parts and not be too surprised at their supposedly irrational behavior.

So, here goes.

The Strategic Apex

What do you think the Strategic Apex, the Central Office, the superintendent, the president, want to do? Of course, the superintendent and the staff's chief concern is *controlling decision making,* so they pull to *centralize all decisions,* to control as much as possible in Mintzberg's model.

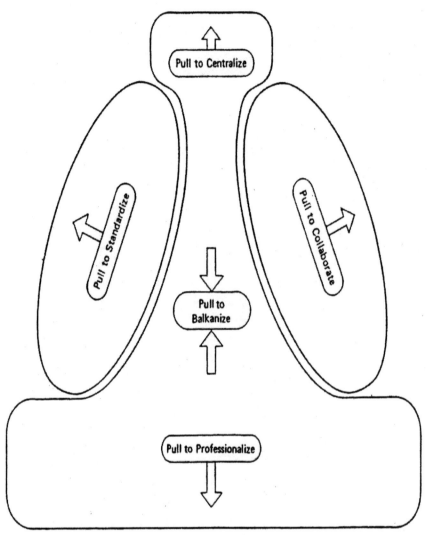

Figure 5.2.   Five Basic Organizational Pulls

Source: Henry Mintzberg, *Structuring of Organizations,* 1st ed. © 1979, p. 302. Reprinted by permission of Pearson Education, Inc., Upper Saddle River, NJ.

Reflective Questions

1. Is this true of your Strategic Apex? Can you picture some of the folks in the Strategic Apex?
2. Is the culture in their office down-to-earth, realistic?
3. Do they seem to have a good grasp of reality? Have their feet on the ground?

4. Do they work on their self-interest—or on yours? Or both? Do you feel they understand you and work in your best interests?
5. Can you give an illustration of an important act, or a recent one to control things?
6. Can you point out recent acts by a former president of the United States that illustrate this?

What we're trying to say here is: what are their main thrusts? Do they work in the best interests of the total school—or mostly their own? If mostly their own, we have problems. If they work for the total system or school, fewer problems will be generated. Often, the Strategic Apex greatly influences how the culture of the organization becomes created.

I remember how removed many people in a Strategic Apex in one district were from classroom reality. We had a severe snowstorm, which prevented lots of teachers from coming into the schools. I was Director of Secondary Education and came up with the not-so-brilliant idea (or, was it?) of asking each of the subject supervisors to sub for their teachers. Many hadn't taught in a classroom for years, and did they have problems! One rather distinguished supervisor decided to retire immediately.

The Middle Line

How about the principals/managers inhabiting the Middle Line? They want *autonomy* to do whatever they want to. So, they try to draw power from the Strategic Apex. Thus, they want to *Balkanize* the organization. That is, they want to be autonomous (like the former Yugoslavia, now Balkan nations, which now have now split into numerous little countries [Slovenia, Serbia, Kosovo, Macedonia]), so they can control their own shops and make their own decisions, do what they want to do without being thwarted by the Strategic Apex.

This is what regional managers do in business and in industry. They try to maximize their autonomy (to try to look good in the eyes of the Strategic Apex—often at the expense of subordinates in the Operating Core).

In large systems they can hide from the central office pretty effectively. In smaller communities this is not so easy to pull off. In the old days, the superintendent, the high school principal, and the football coach played poker on Saturday nights—which tells us the social structure of many small systems.

Principals, especially secondary ones, generally develop good quantities of authority because they often face the public in lots of student activities (athletic games, plays, band performances, booster clubs, etc.), which provides them with frequent community contact. And it generates a good deal of clout for them, which can support their autonomy handsomely.

Reflective Question

Can you think of an illustration or two of principals who have focused on expanding their autonomy?

The Operating Core

How about the Operating Core of teachers and teachers' aides? They want decentralization also, but their pull is to *professionalize*. Teacher literature for decades reflects our desire for increasing professionalization. The National Board of Professional Teacher Standards' increasing popularity attests to this drive, although the route to certification is difficult and laborious. Similarly, in hospitals, this has been the focus of nurses in becoming professionally prestigious Nursing Practitioners. This way, they build prestige and power, (only) partly countering that of physicians.

Probably the major vehicle for teachers' voices to be heard is their drive to unionize. Any organization, such as a school district or a corporation, whose board of directors and administrators has no internal organizational structure (a union, a Concerned Parents' Association, a minority body of some sort) to question its decisions can often run rampant and can make foolish decisions. Thus the value and function of unions focus on their freedom to question decisions and to function as gadflies (often much to the annoyance of leadership).

Teachers' national and state organizations, such as the National Education Association (NEA) and the American Federation of Teachers (AFT) tend to support the drive for increased professionalization mentioned above. NEA national conventions draw well over ten thousand people yearly and they and other organizations (the Association for Supervision and Curriculum Development and the various subject organizations, for example) provide large numbers of sophisticated in-service opportunities for all manner of purposes.

Indeed, many teachers have picked up the idea of getting more in-service experiences as a path to promotion as lead teachers, team leaders, or administrators. I always suggest to teachers who take a course on change strategies to become involved in the most highly visible committees in the schools and district to improve their skills and visibility, and to make appropriate contacts with key decision-making social systems.

The Technostructure

With the advent of huge increases in technology, particularly the computer, technologists occupy an increasingly vital position in schools, districts, companies, and universities. Technocrats tend to want to *standardize* work processes, such as make all computers IBM or IBM clones, or Apples.

Central office people in larger districts want all schools to use the same computer system to schedule, or to report absences, or to use the same report card system. Thus, these folks want to standardize work processes.

While this has appeal, what implications does it have for change in the system or in the school? We'll tackle this below.

Support Staff

And Support Staff? Another key system. According to Mintzberg, they gain the most influence when, because of their expertise, *we need them to collaborate* with us. When they're out sick, almost nothing gets done. Can you remember when a key administrative assistant (formerly called a senior secretary) gets sick for more than a day? Our workplace gets gummed up (since we're stuck without them).

Actually, it's a nightmare. I once had a one-secretary department; the secretary, when she was out for several days, had me answering all phones, trying to remember all sorts of routines that I had not really paid attention to. While people sympathized, I didn't look too good.

TRYING TO SUM UP SO FAR

Don't you find these pulls fascinating, because we can predict fairly well what each component of the organization's interests are, what their likely strategic stance will be for many issues? Take report cards. The Technostructure, to simplify their lives, will try to make all alike, lobbying for that end. In one large nearby district, the techies lobbied for a common middle-school report card to simplify their lives—and actually were successful—much to the chagrin of principals and faculty who wanted to innovate.

Reflective Questions

1. What do you think principals (the Middle Line) want?
2. Do all elementary schools want the same report card? Should they?
3. Should all schools, small learning communities (SLCs), or halls be the same? What does this do to innovation?
4. If a school moves toward a different organization, will it be hamstrung if required to have the same report card?
5. What about discipline? What if a teacher wants to use Kohlberg's Stages of Moral Reasoning (1981) as her basis for discipline?

Many teachers in the Operating Core would love to be able to throw a kid out without having to have principal approval. Actually, such legislation gets considered once in a while. But common sense prevails since interesting problems occur if this is tried.

Reflective Question

How about enrollment?

A progressive principal in a district where I was superintendent actually said that she would not admit any more kids. Can a district permit this autonomy?

SUMMARY

The concept of *pulls*, like many of the ideas and processes described in this book, has considerable value as a tool for us to describe, to analyze, and to predict behavior of people in the five various parts of our organizations. We can then plan to deal more effectively with those behaviors. Thus, chapter 5 presents some useful tools for us to analyze and to predict—which may give us more control of our professional lives—in the process providing the possibility of creating more personal and professional satisfaction.

IMPORTANT TERMS

Kohlberg's Stages of Moral Reasoning—five stages of moral development
Middle Line—mid-level administrators (principals, managers)
Operating Core—the workers (peons) in organizations (teachers, aides)
Strategic Apex—those who run our organization (superintendent, president)
Support Staff—clerical, office folks, custodians
Technostructure—the geeks

6

Adrift, Out of Control, Plunging Over the Waterfall? (OK, Once We Get Our Schools Productive, How Do We Keep Them There?)

At some time in the life cycle of every organization, its ability to succeed in spite of itself runs out.

—Brien's First Law, *Murphy's Law*

ORGANIZATIONAL CYCLES ARE INEVITABLE: PREDICTING AND CONTROLLING THEM ISN'T

In chapters 4 and 5, we asked if you wanted to be able to describe, analyze, and predict accurately what your leaders and those in all of our organizations are going to do. This chapter states that all organizations, like individual humans, have a life cycle of three phases through which they careen uncontrollably. Unless, that is, we know what these phases are—and how to keep the organization in a productive phase of its career.

And—big surprise—each phase has a markedly *different leader* it selects (plus a fourth, a combination of two phases).

This theory describes, analyzes, and predicts both short- and long-range behavior of people in leadership positions—and their organizations. The key trends and patterns it predicts occur inevitably, but they are so gradual and unobtrusive that they often slip by us.

In other words, we focus now on *long-term cycles* that formal organizations *inevitably cycle* through, which are described, analyzed, and predicted by the Tri-Partite Theory of Organizational Succession and Control (Shapiro 2000; Wilson, Byar, Shapiro, and Schell 1969), which impacts their productivity to the point that they lose their way. In the physical world, since all energy systems (solar systems, the brakes in your car, clocks) wear out and run downhill, a term has been developed to describe this—*entropy*. That is, energy systems (certainly what organizations such as schools obviously are) lose their energy—schools, often unfortunately for very, very long periods.

PREDICTING CYCLES IN ORGANIZATIONS

The Tri-Partite Theory of Organizational Succession and Control—And Four Kinds of Leaders

Most of us tend to analyze organizations for relatively short time periods of months or a year or two. A longer focus provides important insights (and, an ability to predict accurately) the *phases* that organizations, including schools, inevitably *career through* in their *careers*. We know that men and women pass through stages as we age—or, maybe, meander through our lives. Researchers (Levinson 1978; Sheehy 1977) discovered that we develop a career as we pass through our life's phases. These insights have found their way into pop culture (middle-age crazies for men, breaking loose for women).

Reflective Question

What if organizations also develop phases in their careers over a relatively long time?

The Tri-Partite Theory states that they do (Shapiro, Benjamin, and Hunt 1995; Wilson, Byar, Shapiro, and Schell 1969). This theory points out that organizations, like physical systems, are *entropic*. That is, as we stated above, we know that all energy systems in the physical world eventually lose their energy, run downhill. Do human systems? This theory states that human organizations, schools, companies, corporations, armies, and nations also lose their energy, eventually running downhill. See figure 6.1.

Reflective Questions

1. Why are so many of our organizations (surely that includes schools) seemingly stuck in the mud, so resistant to change for so long?

Phases of Organizational Change:
Tri-Partite Theory

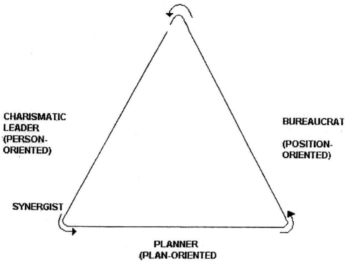

CHARISMATIC
LEADER
(PERSON-
ORIENTED)

BUREAUCRAT

(POSITION-
ORIENTED)

SYNERGIST

PLANNER
(PLAN-ORIENTED

Figure 6.1.   Phases of Organizational Change: Tri-Partite Theory

2. We know that each of us (men and women) go through phases in our lives. Have you ever thought that schools, organizations, have a career, a series of phases through which they pass?
3. Have you ever been in a school that seems mired in red tape, where rules and regulations simply dominate?
4. Or have you ever been in a school or district where exciting things were happening—and in which you had fun?

Everyone can describe organizations seemingly dominated by red tape, rules, and regulations. The school or district or company can be described best as bureaucratically dominated, with the principal or superintendent or president more of a caretaker, maintaining order, more a tinkerer than a developer. Essentially, nothing happens; routine dominates. Its mission has been forgotten, with people looking back to a mythical golden age when it was exciting to live in it. People at the top are careful to follow the rules to protect themselves and are fearful of making changes, so the place is locked into routine, status quo, stagnation.

Dozens of organizations illustrate this, from Chrysler and Ford, to Washington, D.C.'s schools, to IBM (who thought mainframes would dominate the world), to General Motors (which had a 50 percent share of the auto market once to its well under 21 percent today), to many state departments, local schools, and districts locked into the status quo.

The Person-Oriented Phase of the Organization's Career—
Enter the Charismatic Leader

At some point, the board of directors, or board of education, or chief executive, becomes seriously concerned that disaster is looming for the total organization or school (e.g., three straight years of failing state tests). They begin to look for a dynamic individual with vision, energy, ideas, and charisma to break the school out of its funk and to reenergize it. Such a *charismatic* person energizes people. People come out of the woodwork, attracted by this person's vision and energy.

Such a person brings hope for the future, generating loyalty. This state of an organization's career we call *person-orientation*. The leader? The *charismatic*.

Examples? Mahatma and Indiri Gandhi in India, John Fitzgerald Kennedy, President Barack Obama, Michael Jordan, and Generals Robert E. Lee, Eisenhower, and Patton. With regard to civil rights, Martin Luther King; religion, Billy Graham, Christ, Moses, Mohammed.

With regard to education, John Dewey; Robert Maynard Hutchins, president of the University of Chicago and champion of the Great Books; and Al Shanker, former president of the American Federation of Teachers, come to mind.

The charismatic leader's role is fascinating, since this type of leader breaks the organization out of its doldrums, its mind-numbing routines, by expressing with ideas the hopes, aspirations, and interests of doing significant things professionally and personally. Such a person excites the imagination of large numbers of people and can lead them to exciting ventures. Such leadership facilitates generating large numbers of initiatives, usually uncoordinated, to which many flock.

People express a great deal of hope since the future is wide open in comparison with the scenario painted above. People actually like being there. They feel excited, energized.

Actions tend to be short-range and exciting, with people developing hosts of ideas, initiatives, and plans, often uncoordinated. In this person-oriented phase of its career, the organization is at its most dynamic. Unfortunately, when asked if people have lived in such a phase, usually less than one-third respond affirmatively.

Reflective Question

Are all religions started by charismatics?

The Planning Phase: The Planner, and Plan-Orientation

Usually, the person-oriented phase of an organization's career tends to be short—two to four years. People begin to tire of the action and want more stability. Or the charismatic may become attracted to another organization that wants the pizzazz and publicity the leader generates, or the leader gets shot out of the saddle, leaving followers anxious to retain some of the later ideas. They try to recruit someone who can take these later ideas and fashion them into a plan. So the organization generally unwittingly selects a *planner* to head up the next phase of its career.

Reflective Questions

1. Have you ever worked in a school or district that was headed by a planner?
2. How did the planner operate? Was this leader as charismatic as the former leader?

Obviously, planners come in different shapes and sizes, ranging from someone who focuses on one idea (block scheduling, improved report cards) to those who advocate system-wide and systemic change (decentralization into SLCs, or middle schools, or continuous progress, full-service schools, constructivist teaching).

Examples of planners are not as evident as charismatic leaders, since most planners tend to work behind the scenes and do not exhibit as much charisma. Douglas MacArthur was a planner, as were Omar Bradley, Bill Gates, Lee Iacocca, and Donald Trump. Martin Luther King and the two Gandhis should be mentioned. We have more difficulty in citing planners in education. Dale Parnell, the founder of the Tech-Prep movement in community colleges, is one example, as was Al Shanker.

Whom do *you* nominate?

Plans can range from simple (changing the report card) to complex, such as decentralizing by converting a school into SLCs, moving into a middle school, restructuring the district (three- or four-year high school), developing portfolios, etc. So plans can range from short range and small to comprehensive and long term. Moving into team and/or constructivist teaching represents a multiyear endeavor.

The plan guides and harnesses the organization's energies, focus, resources. In comparison with the person-oriented view of the future, which is wide open, plan-orientation focuses on achieving the plan. Action is long-range in comparison with the person-oriented phase, which can result in people becoming loyal to the plan, contrasting with the person-oriented phase where loyalty is to the leader.

Reflective Questions

1. Have you ever been in an organization dominated by a plan?
2. What was it like? How were priorities set?
3. How long did it last? (Key Question)

The Fate of Plans and the Planning Phase

Most plans follow an inevitable, fixed, and fateful career or template—unless one knows the pattern. And therein lies its Achilles heel. Usually, a plan garners a good deal of support if involvement is heavy and if a minority doesn't force it upon an acquiescent majority.

However, as time passes, the day-to-day, bit-by-bit incremental nature of decision making focusing on immediate crises and conditions tends to drift slowly away from holding the plan aloft as a prism guiding all action and resources. As time unfolds, new people enter who have not participated in its development and implementation, and so are not necessarily passionate advocates, while the original pioneers leave. The new give lip service to the plan, but usually feel less loyalty.

After two or three years, the plan begins to be honored more in the breach than in actually guiding actions. By five years, the plan has slid out of our consciousness and gets brought up by old-timers reminiscing about the Good Old Days. As an example, I was once hired by a prominent midwestern university lab school to be a fieldwork supervisor and core teacher, teaching language arts and social studies in the seventh grade in a brand new building built for that purpose. Oddly, I returned eight years later to interview for the small city's assistant superintendency; so of course, I looked up my old friends. By this time, my colleagues and I had developed the Tri-Partite Theory. Therefore, I did not ask the naïve question, "What happened to Core?" Instead, I asked predictively, "Hey, guys, when did Core die?" to a group really taken aback. No one answered at first—no one knew. Core had simply slipped away; people had a difficult time pinning down when it had stopped.

Reflective Question

How can we explain this certain outcome?

More organizational dynamics explain these change processes. As people in organizations develop their plans, they set up rules and regulations to achieve their goals. They begin to establish carefully crafted job descriptions, designed for the same purpose. Red tape flourishes and begins to rule the roost, with secretaries even telling top administrators what to do and what they cannot do. Slowly, spontaneity, creativity, and vigor gets squeezed out.

In this process, the plan begins to lose its vision on people's imagination and day-to-day actions. Priorities change, and by this time, the planner, like the charismatic leader, a nomad, looks around for new challenges. Or she has left for a school looking for a plan.

The Position-Oriented Phase of the Organization's Career—
Enter the Bureaucrat

By this time the planner has been succeeded by a person whose main focus is to stabilize—in short, a bureaucrat who generally likes red tape and regulations, often to increase personal power. The great upswing of hope generated in the person-oriented phase has long disappeared, since the organization tends to become backward-looking, pointing to past glories and achievements. The bureaucratic leader tends to be a stabilizer, or a tinkerer, who has problems breaking out of the box. This type of leader becomes a prisoner of the box—or creates the box itself to feel safe.

When crises occur, the organization shudders and copes with symptoms, rather than focusing on long-range creative solutions. Often such an administrator will be authoritarian, focusing on control, a Theory X person. Thus, people, at best loyal to the position, are *position-oriented*. Examples? President George H. W. Bush, who noted that he would look at his in-box, take care of it, and leave.

Many ask how long various phases last. Unfortunately, this third one is the longest, since often the superintendents will hire a principal who is safe, someone who does not want to, or cannot, rock the boat. Most organizations seem to reside in this phase—often for a long time. If a school or district hires an insider, they're usually going to stay in the bureaucratic phase, since they're looking for stability.

The Synergist

Once in a blue moon, we can find someone who is both charismatic *and* a planner, a *synergist*. You will note that several names are repeated, including President Obama (who observers note ran the best campaign they ever saw), General MacArthur, Robert E. Lee, Lee Iacocca, Robert Maynard Hutchins, Dale Parnell. Obviously, Mahatma Gandhi fits, as does Martin Luther King.

Reflective Question

Whom do you nominate?

Synergists are exceedingly useful in breaking out of doldrums in which a position-oriented school or district finds itself. This rarity combines both charisma *and* planning, so we have a real package. Since they are rare, an alternative approach would be to develop a synergistic staffing plan as a possibility, with a charismatic leader and a planner (providing they can work together). They have to be mature enough to deal with jealousy that can arise when one receives more kudos. Both are essential.

Obviously, examples of this arise when teams have coaches exemplifying these talents, as with the Chicago Bears of the early 1980s, when Mike Ditka was the head coach and Buddy Ryan handled the famous "46" defense. Presently? How about Barack Obama as President and Hillary Clinton as Secretary of State?

Reflective Question

How to beat this entropy?

Better replan every two to three years, or the plan will be lost. This is discussed in the case study presented in chapters 11 and 12.

SUMMARY

In this chapter, the third on what makes organizations work, we dealt at some length with the three phases of the cycle that organizations (including schools) inevitably career through, predicted by the Tri-Partite Theory of Organizational Change and Succession. The theory predicts that all formal organizations career through three phases in order: Person-orientation, Plan-orientation, and Position-orientation, with a leadership style associated with each phase: a Charismatic leader, followed by a Planner, succeeded by a Bureaucrat. And once in a blue moon, we get a combination of the first two, a Synergist.

Thus, chapter 6 presents some useful tools for us to analyze and to predict to control our professional lives, providing the possibility of creating more personal and professional satisfaction in the process.

IMPORTANT TERMS

Assumptions—starting points in everyone's thinking
Entropy—a theory that organizations, like physical entities, experience loss of energy, purpose
Synergist—a leader who combines charisma with planning talent; a relative rarity
Tri-Partite Theory of Organizational Succession and Control—a theory that organizations cycle through a career of three phases with four associated leadership styles:

- Charismatic
- Planner
- Synergist
- Bureaucrat

7

Power and Its Uses: Sink or Swim

Knowledge is power.

—Sir Frances Bacon, *Meditationes Sacrae*, 1597

The purpose of getting power is to give it away.

—Aneurin Bevan, 1945–1960, 1962, British Prime Minister

Any book dealing with leadership must deal with how to use and how to work with power—and particularly, how not to lose it.

ORGANIZATION OF THIS SHORT CHAPTER

We Westerners have been having a love-hate relationship with power for centuries—no, for over three millennia, since at least the days of Homer and probably way before that. We'll first deal with Barnard's shrewd understanding of power and authority, then with Weber, who threw in the idea of influence, take a brief look at sources of power, and turn to a sociologist, Robert Bierstedt, for his astute and simple formulation of power and how it applies to everyday life in our organizations, including our families. Last, we'll look at implications for survival and effective function.

Reflective Questions

1. So, now, what must people in leadership positions (which include principals, teachers—even parents) understand about power and its relatives, influence and authority, to function successfully in our schools?
2. And in our families?

This is essentially a survival question since those who do not grasp the uses of power, authority, and influence and act very weakly will have people shortly running all over them, and those who become power-mad bullies and dictators will generate opposition that can eventually wash over them like a tsunami, either drowning them or leaving them high and dry (and out of the school).

So, let's start.

BARNARD, THE FATHER OF ADMINISTRATIVE THOUGHT

Virtually everyone—even today—believes that the authority of anyone in a leadership position comes from their superior. The principal gets his power from a grant from the superintendent who in turn is empowered by the Board of Education.

Wrong!

Barnard (1938) turned this thinking on its head by proposing that people in leadership positions build their authority and power because their subordinates *accept their communications.* The subordinate *perceives* the communication as authoritative, coming from a superior, and *accepts* it.

Voila! The person in the position of leadership now has power and authority (and also influence).

This comprises a major change from believing that we get our power from those above us to understanding that we acquire it from our *communications being accepted by subordinates.* Suddenly, we've moved into communications theory and group dynamics to begin to grasp the tendrils, the strings of authority and power.

Some change!

Barnard then lays out four conditions for authority to exist in organizations (and these apply to our families, as well).

1. The communication must be understood by subordinates.
2. The communication must be consistent with the subordinates' perceptions of the purposes of the organization.

3. Subordinates have to perceive the communication to be consistent with their own purposes.
4. Subordinates have to be able to carry out the communication both physically and mentally.

Let's see how these play out—the enormously far-reaching implications of these apparently simple statements. First, if people in leadership positions are to develop power and authority, people must *believe* they have it. So, we must be aware of all these four conditions. We must communicate directly and clearly (another principle of Barnard).

The key for Barnard is that subordinates have to *accept communications* without full, rational analysis of the options available. Subordinates accept decisions because they believe that the leaders have the *right* to make such decisions or communications.

If they accept it—we have power and authority. If not—we have neither. All of a sudden, we are thrust into people's heads, that is, how people think and make meanings from situations. If the decisions and communications are not accepted, we have a catastrophic situation, since we can no longer lead. People may actually decide not to accept orders from us. And this kind of nonacceptance can spread. If it does, we are finished. Parents whose adolescent kids decide not to accept their authority are cooked.

Illustrations of this sudden loss of power are instances of high drama. During the Vietnam War, officers who pushed too hard and didn't build support of and from the troops, in some instances were fragged (murdered) by their own men, a rather unpleasant end.

Reflective Questions

1. In the Iraq war, some Americans tortured prisoners at Abu Ghraib. Which of Barnard's four principles were violated?
2. What examples can you dredge up to illustrate these principles?

COMPARING POWER, AUTHORITY, AND INFLUENCE

We've taken a look at one way of approaching the phenomena of power and authority, but have only glanced sideways at influence. To deal with that, we explore Max Weber's (1946) ideas. Weber, a German sociologist who worked in the latter two decades of the nineteenth century and the first two of the twentieth century, tried to capture the relationships among power, authority, and influence (see Figure 7.1).

Weber focused on *influence* upon others' behavior, which he split into *voluntary* and *involuntary* compliance. The latter, involuntary compliance,

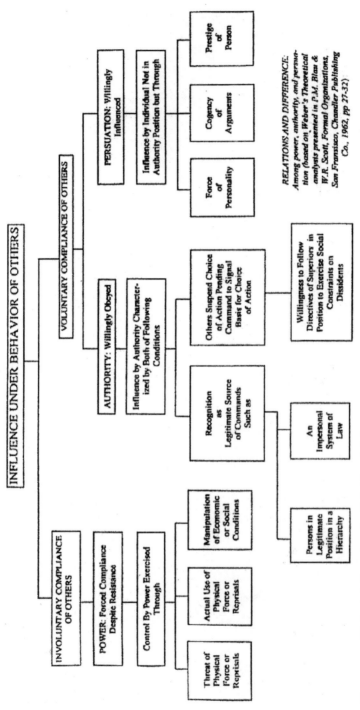

Figure 7.1.   Weber's Influence under Behavior of Others

Source: Based on Max Weber's Theoretical Analysis presented in P. M. Blau and W. R. Scott, *Formal Organizations* (San Francisco: Chandler Publishing, 1962), pp. 27–32. Reprinted by permission of Pearson Education.

rests on power, forced compliance, for Weber. Power, in turn, rests on threats, actual use of physical force, or manipulation of social or economic conditions, such as threats of being fired, or actual firings as warnings.

Usually, this is infrequently used in leadership nowadays.

On the other hand, authority and influence are based on *voluntary compliance*. Authority is willingly obeyed because people in the organization recognize it as coming from the superior's position and, therefore, treat the authority as legitimate, and, therefore, do not search for alternatives to any communication.

Persuasion is a major factor in involuntary compliance because it comes from recognizing the other person's charisma, cogency of arguments, or prestige. In Weber's view it pays to be respected and prestigious, in short, to be a reference person.

Reflective Questions

1. Is it clear why most people's decisions to go along are usually based on persuasion?
2. And on the influence of the person in a leadership position?

SOURCES OF POWER: FRENCH AND RAVEN (AND OTHERS)

French and Raven (1959) added considerably to our understanding of the fields of power, authority, and influence by digging into their sources. Additionally, I've added a couple from Lambert et al. (1996), Dunlap and Goldman (1991), the last three from Bolman and Deal (1991), and two of my own.

- Legitimate or position power—one has this from the position as principal.
- Reward power—wears off rapidly because teachers want more pay, kids more treats.
- Expertise, knowledge—respect accrues because you know things. Statisticians because we and they know we are statistical morons, budget gurus because we realize we are highly deficient (read, morons).
- Tradition—really, based largely on one's position, which has a long history (the president of the United States, the priest, the principal). We respect the office, and usually the occupant.
- Referential power—power, influence because the individual is highly respected, considered a person of great substance. This has to be earned over time. Who are your reference persons?

- Charismatic power—usually, the charismatic person wins elections. President Kennedy's power lasts even today. A major power and influence base.
- Love—mostly seen as one's favorite teacher. Lasts a lifetime.
- Modeling—after which teacher do you model yourself? Which parent? Which leader? Usually, we may be somewhat unaware of modeling anyone until we get introspective.
- Facilitative—from Dunlap and Goldman (1991). Group dynamics here.
- Alliances and networks—the smart person builds them. Helps to build networks of friends and allies.
- Access to and control of agendas—access to decision-making arenas. The person who controls the minutes, particularly if they are done publicly, accrues considerable influence and power.
- Control of meanings and symbols—crucial in establishing the subculture of the group or social system or organization.

This last point is key. If one can influence the organization in its process of creating meanings, establishing values, and creating common symbols, one has a great deal of influence. "Collaboration in developing common meanings is the key to constructivist use of power" (Shapiro 2008, 144).

To that can be added Lambert et al.'s (1996) perception that developing *positive supportive relationships* underlies the essence of building leadership, because people in leadership positions who can build a shared vision and personal commitment facilitate the development of their power and influence (but only if that is not their purpose).

SOCIAL POWER—ROBERT BIERSTEDT

Our final insight comes from sociologist Bierstedt (1950), who thought about social power.

Reflective Questions

1. What do we mean by social power?
2. This gets at a fundamental question: what are organizations?

Bierstedt and any good sociologist perceive organizations as *social* entities, actually as *socially constructed realities*. What do we mean by this? As pointed out in chapter 3, when we form organizations, immediately positions, roles, and role expectations are created, with some positions having more power, authority, and influence than others (choirgirl, choral leader, pastor).

Bierstedt's formulations follow:

Power is institutionalized authority,
Authority, in turn, rests on the capacity to apply sanctions; and
Sanctions are stored force.

Pretty short. Even pithy (and full of vinegar).

Interpretations and Applications of Bierstedt

So, social power rests on one's *capacity* to apply force. And therein lies the limits of using power. If we use it and it fails—we are done in. We suddenly have absolutely no power and certainly no authority. Even our influence wanes abruptly. Power, therefore, consists of a *capacity to employ force*. Power, therefore, is *potential*. It consists of *stored force*, the ability to use force.

This is why militaries are extremely cautious actually to use force, because if it fails, their power evaporates.

Reflective Question

Can you think of an example of this? (Vietnam? Authorizing use of nuclear weapons?)

Implications of Bierstedt (and Perhaps our Other Sources)

Anyone thinking about Bierstedt's ideas has to consider any use of force or authority very, very carefully. Because if we use it and it doesn't work, we will lose a great deal. Thus, statements of any intention to use power must be followed through if challenged. We cannot wuss out of such a challenge. People must be absolutely certain that the person with the power will use it if challenged.

My approach as an administrator when I saw a challenge being contemplated was to say, "Look, I'm not threatening or challenging you. If you do this, then I will do the following. It's your choice." This was usually enough to head off foolish confrontations without loss of face for everyone.

Many *myths* have arisen about power. Lambert cites Macy (1994–1995) as suggesting a few that, hopefully, this analysis has demolished:

- Power is a scarce commodity—only some people have it.
- Power and authority are vested only in positioned leaders.
- For me to have power, I have to reduce yours (because power is limited in organizations).

- Power consists of forcing one's will on others and reducing choices for them.
- Building defenses makes us powerful.
- Having power gives one the ability to legislate meaning and to fix identity.

In the next chapter we talk about various ways to look at leadership. One approach, constructivist leadership, focuses on the necessity of forming positive relationships. We will see that involving people, building positive relationships with them, and, equally, building trust become the foundations for building power, authority, and influence.

We now have major keys for professional and personal action and interaction: *building relationships becomes the key for building leadership.*

SUMMARY

We now have the understanding to be able to build our power, authority, and influence. We've looked at various formulations from Barnard, Weber, and Bierstedt for insights. We've used French and Raven and a handful of others to root out the sources of power. And we've looked at some of the implications of how to use these forces constructively, which are crucial for survival in organizations (and even families).

IMPORTANT TERMS

Authority—based on communications, following Barnard's formulation

Influence—either voluntary or involuntary compliance, according to Weber

Power—the capacity to employ stored force

Reference person—a person with great prestige and respect to whom we listen

8

Leadership—The Impact of the Honcho (If We Find a Honcho to Diagnose and to Steer Us Through Shoals)

The secret of success is constancy of purpose.

—Benjamin Disraeli, June 24, 1872

Do you have a constancy of purpose?

—W. Edwards Deming, February 1981 (to Ford executives)

The proper function of government is to strengthen the levels below.

—Clarence Darrow

INTRODUCTION AND ORGANIZATION

Leadership is crucial to success—its lack greases the slippery road to disaster (at least in Western Civilization). It's a source of

- drive or neutral (or even reverse)
- energy or inertia
- ideas or know-nothingism
- inclusion or exclusion
- involvement or alienation
- enthusiasm or despair

- expansion or contraction
- leading toward constructive goals or going astray
- building or destroying social capital
- In short, leadership can build or, equally, can implode any organization. Want a quick example of the latter?

Reflective Questions

1. Can you think of any organization that has imploded? (Hint: the Republican Party under George W. Bush, Enron).
2. Any others? How about Fanny Mae and Freddy Mac? General Motors?

Leadership can be looked at in a number of ways. For our purposes, let's analyze first how it works, its dynamics, by starting to treat leadership as a social function and a social process. Then, we'll look at the social functions of organizations and schools, since some of these functions may be startling— even uncomfortable. The impact of the social functions of organizations and schools with only three role options possible for all leaders is next.

Leadership as a system of behavior is next viewed followed by the invaluable contribution of Chester I. Barnard (1938) to thinking about the functions of the executive. Next, viewing organizations from the viewpoint of their inevitably developing a career of three phases though which they usually careen uncontrollably informs us about the behavior of leaders in each of the three phases. Next, research findings regarding the necessity of facilitating establishing a philosophy and positive relationships to create an effective subculture with trust are treated. Another study dealing with teachers' perceptions of leadership is presented and the value of decentralizing through SLCs and PLCs is discussed.

In this next section, such issues as empowerment through involvement and power are pointed out as are references from preceding chapters dealing with images of organizations, the pulls exerted from various parts of the organization as noted by Mintzberg (1979), and organizational cycles. We end with a summary, even some conclusions and, perhaps, some grist for contemplation.

THE DYNAMICS OF LEADERSHIP

Leadership as a Social Function and a Social Process

Reflective Question

What do we mean by "social function" and "social process"?

Leadership occurs in a social context, obviously. Robinson Caruso could exert no leadership until Friday appeared—and accepted his attempts at leadership. Equally obviously, organizations are social in nature since they consist of people interacting. They also are constructed by us. And do they consist of realities! Just talk to people who've lost their jobs and even their homes due to any recession. That's an extremely harsh reality.

OK, we've just now established that *organizations are socially constructed realities.*

And the whole function of leadership is one social function in organizations, among others (see below). As a matter of fact, leadership is also socially constructed (Komives, Lucas, and McMahon 1998). An illustration comparing and contrasting the Americans' and the Fox Indians' grant of authority to those in leadership positions makes the point most decisively.

In the American culture, the position of leader is *granted* to someone formally (although informal leadership in organizations and social situations exist [Follett 1924]). That leadership and grant of authority can be executed through the lifetime of the individual's residence in the position. That is, the *grant* to use the *key of authority* is permanent (unless the person really screws up mightily [such as Nixon]).

The Fox Indians, however, operated totally differently. The Fox had no concept of *vertical* authority, so nobody could exert even a scintilla of authority. If someone was chosen by the elders to lead a war party, he had to cajole colleagues to join him. They could decide whether or not to follow his suggestions (not orders), or they could leave at any time. His grant to use the key of leadership only lasted until the action occurred, which even then was limited—and then it was over. In short, the key to use authority was extremely limited and very strongly distrusted (Hanvey 1963). It really verged into influence only.

The Fox key was given to the *function* (hunting), not to the *person or position*, as in the West. Huge difference! For the Fox Indians, personal autonomy overrode everything, much to the astonishment and consternation of Westerners. The Fox believed that everyone was highly capable and never developed a need or a provision for authority in their culture. The closest model or theory of leadership that honors that approach is constructivist leadership (Lambert et al. 1995; Shapiro 2008) where people in leadership positions operate more as colleagues than as superiors. The leader is considered neither the authority nor the wisest.

It's easy to conclude with this example that the nature of authority underlying leadership as well as leadership itself may be constructed very differently in different cultures and social systems. Leadership and its underpinning of authority clearly are *socially constructed*, that is, bounded by all sorts of role expectations and norms that cultures create over time (concede an election loss gracefully rather than being a sore loser, nor plan a coup, never look uncertain or depressed, act professionally, listen carefully to everyone).

The Social Functions of Organizations and Schools

Leadership develops in organizations as part of the *social process of people interacting* with each other. As a matter of fact, leadership comprises one of the major and indispensable social functions of organizations in complex Western organizations. Without it, usually little or nothing gets accomplished.

Examples of other social functions of organizations include providing distribution of resources, that is, establishing avenues to make a living, making decisions and structures involving development of consent and governance (political parties, government), providing emotional security, as well as socializing people both into the culture and into the organization itself. Some organizations' social functions include providing arenas for people to meet their social, recognition, and recreation needs (health clubs at the workplace).

The social functions of schools (Shapiro, Benjamin, and Hunt 1995) for example, include a social sorting function, much to the dismay of most Americans. Schools usually develop hierarchical social structures so that kids know where they fit into the society and culture of the school from the most respected statuses (National Honor Society) to those at the bottom rungs. Kids rapidly become aware of the social class structure of the school, particularly in middle and high schools. This informs kids regarding where they stand in the American culture's social class system. Schools also have a warehousing function in that they keep kids off the street by filling their time. What do we use to perform this purpose? Study halls.

Schools socialize kids and adults by inculcating people into the immense number of symbols in the culture, as well as its norms, expectations, role expectations, customs, and practices. In school kids learn to behave like kindergartners and, later, adolescents (pointing out a problem home schooling faces to resolve). Some cynics note that failure is designed to enhance the value of the diploma; schools that eliminate social promotion increase their dropout rates. These social functions are illustrative, since numerous others have been created, such as schools as vehicles for social ascent, transmitting the social heritage, etc.

Impact of Social Functions of Organizations/Schools on Leadership— Only Three Options

Reflective Questions

1. With which of these three options are you most comfortable? Why?
2. Which is most effective in generating change?

These social functions of organizations and, particularly, schools, exert an impact on leadership. Those in leadership positions who do not have a "big picture" perception of this frame of three potential lines of action in which they can view these social functions are often doomed to forge ahead and to implement them without rationally examining them to make decisions regarding which to implement and which to change.

Social Function One: Change Little—Go Along to Get Along

So, unthinkingly plunging into the vast ocean called schools dooms the leader merely to swim along with what has developed. VanMaanen and Schein (1979) point to three choices for leaders entering any organization (including the one of custodianship) where the incomer learns and accepts the expectations of the position in the social system of the organization and the strategies normally utilized to achieve those expectations. In this approach, the leader (who hardly leads) "goes along to get along." For example, General Motors' refusal for years to develop fuel-efficient cars is an illustration. In education, administrators who refuse to consider decentralizing into teams and/or SLCs to improve teaching and learning despite the clear research benefits are another.

Social Function Two: Limited Change—Content Innovation Usually

The second option available comprises content innovation, in which alternative strategies are selected instead of continuing present practices. In this choice, changes in the base of knowledge or the practices and strategies are made. The new leader does not accept the huge rash of norms, practices, beliefs, and myths of people in the social system the leader enters. Changes in reading programs found by research to be more effective would be an example. Decisions to move from passive into active and team-based learning are others. To improve teaching and learning is another.

Social Function Three: Role Innovation

The third choice? That's the most interesting, the most creative, and provides the most opportunity to change and to revitalize the organization/school. This third option consists of role innovation, in which the new leader redefines his/her role by changing its purpose, its focus, and its expectations. VanMaanen and Schein note "a genuine attempt is made by the role holder to redefine the ends for which the role functions. . ." (1979, 229).

Changing the structure of the school by decentralizing into teams and SLCs to make schools become more personal comprises major changes, requiring long-range strategies. Establishing a school-wide or district-wide curriculum generating structure comprises another. (See chapter 4, "Hidden

Eddies That Drive Us Off Course: Metaphors and Images of Organizations (Which Often Dominate Our Thinking) and a Curriculum-Steering Task Force That Generates Controlled Change as a Routine," for example.)

Deming and Reform

Recent literature in industry and education seems to support these second and third approaches, including Deming (1982), among others. Deming's whole approach calls for improving the organization's *system*, obviously referring to the seventh of his fourteen steps. Deming is quite clear about the function of leadership when he states emphatically, "The basic cause of sickness in American industry and resulting unemployment is failure of top management to manage" (p. 1).

He further notes that *the system* is responsible for 85 percent of all quality problems, and that management has to lead in changing systems and the processes that create the organization's problems. The Tri-Partite Theory (chapter 6) speaks very directly to this in citing the Charismatic, Planner, and Synergistic leaders.

Leadership as a System of Behavior

We've talked about leadership as a social process and as a social function. It's useful also to note that sociologists consider leadership as a *behavior system* or a *system of behavior*.

Reflective Question

What do we mean by leadership as a system of behavior?

That's easy.

Just close your eyes and think of the shelves of books on leadership in any bookstore, such as Barnes and Noble. Huge numbers of books are published on leadership (although fewer than a dozen theories of leadership have been developed [the Tri-Partite Theory of Organizational Change and Succession, which was presented in chapter 6, a brief summary of which will be made shortly, is one of those few]). These books all look at, analyze, and even try to predict the behavior of people in leadership positions. Leadership has become a pop culture phenomenon. And virtually all those books focus on improving our behavior as leaders.

Voila! They are treating leadership as a system of behavior that you and I, if we're smart enough to read and to buy their books, can improve. As a matter of fact, if you can dream up a different slant to publish on leadership, you may have a bestseller (whether it's based on research or not. See English's research [2002] on Covey's Seven Habits of Effective Leaders).

Further support for VanMaanen and Schein's third alternative of major role innovation is supported by research on Chaos Theory (Gleick 1987; Pascale 1990). Their approach contends that leaders, to be successful with systemic and constructive change, need to create focused dissonance, rather than the American Holy Grail of Harmony. Pascale even proposes "the tension (dynamic synthesis) between contradictory opposites as the engine of self-renewal. It (renewal) is predicated on the notion that disequilibrium is a better strategy for adaptation and survival than order and equilibrium" (1990, 24).

Reflective Questions

1. Do you want more support for this strange idea?
2. What is your reaction?

Well, Pascale elaborates (are you surprised?):

Over the past fifteen years, natural scientists have grappled with a "paradigm shift" because evolutionary processes testify to the paradoxical way in which fluctuation creates equilibrium. Traditionally, fluctuation was seen as disturbing equilibrium. Yet, as the previously cited findings suggest, order based on equilibrium is vulnerable to destruction (owing to the stagnation and absence of adaptation), whereas order based on disequilibrium has a much higher probability of being maintained. (1990, 108)

Reflective Question

What are we to make of this?

Obviously, this runs counter to usual common sense and intuition, which in much of our thinking strives for harmony. Oddly, these insights of Chaos Theory support those of the Tri-Partite Theory, which places a great deal of emphasis on the planning function of organizations.

And as we have seen in chapter 6, it is crucial for moving an organization into a more productive phase of its career, after being broken out of its senescent and essentially dead third phase in position-orientation by a charismatic leader. Particularly, chapter 4 and the last chapter, chapter 14, "Summing Up," present systems and structures that *generate change as a routine*, thereby essentially keeping the school in a state of controlled change, a sort of *disequilibriumized equilibrium*.

The next section deals with three indispensable functions of organizations.

Barnard's Functions of the Executive—Fundamental Thinking

Reflective Question

Why Barnard?

Chester Barnard (1938) is widely considered the father of contemporary administration. Instead of asking about the purposes of administration (really, leadership), he shifted the frame he used into asking what are the *indispensable functions* of those in leadership positions.

- The first is to facilitate *developing a common purpose.*
- The second is to *establish a system of communication* with as direct channels as possible.
- The third is to *establish a system of cooperation* to achieve the common purpose.

This sounds rather simple, but it takes a good deal of thought and work. If any organization does not have a common purpose, it goes nowhere—or, in all directions (which is nowhere). And, these three indispensable functions are interlocking. We cannot achieve one without the others. A system of communication is completely necessary to establish a common purpose. Otherwise, how are the members of the organization (read school, family, corporation, platoon) to know about and to implement the common goals? Lack of effective communication is often a norm as our organizations get larger, which blocks accomplishing goals and objectives, so that, almost inevitably, large organizations shudder to a halt (Washington, D.C., schools, Chrysler).

Similarly, establishing a system of cooperation is absolutely indispensable to achieving common purposes. Unless people learn to cooperate—and want to—they cannot accomplish the goals that the people in the organization set.

An illustration? A kindergarten.

The little guys have a difficult time subordinating their wants to play concertedly with even one other child. It usually starts out as parallel play. So, to an outsider's eyes, kindergartens seem like chaos personified. Really structured teachers have a difficult time in such a setting. As the kids get older and more socialized, they begin to subordinate their wants to the norms established to run the operation.

The American culture focuses so heavily on competition that it often overrides the need for people in organizations to cooperate to achieve common goals. But note that teams, to be effective, must cooperate. Members of a front line of a football team must learn to work together to achieve their goals.

Reflective Question

Does pitting schools based on choice (charter schools, magnets) against each other to build their enrollment facilitate their desire to cooperate with other schools, or does it reduce it?

It's important to be realistic in looking at motivation in our current accountability-crazed climate. The British have found to their dismay that competitive schools reduce cooperation with each other. If we set up a contest to recognize a teacher (Teacher of the Year, National Board), it exacerbates jealousy and resentment. "Why don't you send that new kid to *her?*"

A Major Barnardian Function of Leadership

So, one function of leadership behavior is *to facilitate establishing plans to accomplish the goals* developed by members of the organization.

The Tri-Partite Theory of Organizational Change and Succession

We'll mention this briefly, since we dealt with it more fully in chapter 6, "Adrift, Out of Control . . . The Inevitability of Organizational Cycles." The essence of the Tri-Partite Theory (Shapiro 2000; Wilson et al. 1969) is that organizations, like individuals, careen almost inevitably through a career of three phases: a Person-oriented phase, followed by Plan-orientation, and last, a Position-orientation. Each phase, interestingly, is led by a different style of leadership.

Person-orientation is called that because the leader is charismatic in nature (Bill Clinton), followed by a Planner (Alan Greenspan), and last, Position-orientation is led (if you want to call it that) by a Bureaucrat (President George H. W. Bush), who does little or merely tinkers while the organization slowly slides into senescence, just drifts, to be rescued eventually by a charismatic leader who revitalizes the organization. Once in a blue moon we get a synergist, who combines charismatic leadership with the capacity to plan (Barack Obama, Warren Buffet).

This theory, oddly, is similar to a physical theory, which states that all energy systems run downhill, that is, they are *entropic.* That is, all energy systems in the physical world decay in time.

Reflective Question

Do all social systems, all organizations, all schools decay?

That's why I call this the Great Dismal Theory, because it predicts that even if we get an organization into a highly productive phase of its career (the first two, obviously), it will almost inevitably lose its way, lose its plan, and just drift in the third phase—that is—unless we know enough to *replan carefully* in two or three years to reestablish a plan to reenergize and redirect the system.

Like all social phenomena, this theory exposes a dark side, since charismatic leaders can be moral (Gandhi) or amoral (Hitler), lead toward destructive goals or toward constructive ends (profit first over concern for employees, such as GM's vs. Toyota's and Honda's CEOs).

Reflective Question

How can we tell in what stage an organization is in currently?

One key is to look at the leadership. Another key is to ask whether an organization develops a *plan*. If no plan, it goes nowhere, drifts. Another diagnostic question to ask is: did you ever have a plan? And, then you wait. If they respond, "Oh, sure, we had a plan five years ago when we really had a great school" we have the answer. The school is resting in the third phase—not going anywhere.

Interestingly, the Tri-Partite ties into Barnard's thinking in that he clearly wants organizations to develop a plan, which Barnard thinks is the hallmark of an effective leader.

MORE DYNAMICS OF LEADERSHIP

Develop a Coherent Philosophy

To create a plan it is extremely useful to develop a *coherent philosophy*, which, if held aloft as a prism to guide policies and actions, can be crucial—no—decisive in guiding leadership and members of the school/organization in their daily decision-making (Barnard 1938; Isaacson 2004; Shapiro 2008). We are guided by our *frames of reference* (a set or system of ideas which orient or give particular meaning to our thinking [Mish 1988]), and which Alan Greenspan called our ideology. Isaacson (2004), who moved her large elementary school into one that practiced constructivist teaching, was convinced that developing a constructivist philosophy by which to make all decisions was essential to their effectiveness. It focused all their actions—and new teachers bought into this because it was embedded in the culture of the school and teachers' practices.

Additionally, teachers recognized that subthemes under the constructivist philosophy were also crucial; these consisted of problem-solving, heavy-duty reflecting to improve practice, creating a risk-free environment, and focusing on developing learner-centered activities. Teachers' perceptions in Isaacson's study revealed three dimensions of leadership and six in teachers as leaders (discussed in chapters 11 and 12).

Lambert et al. (1995), who was the founder of investigating and developing the field of constructivist leadership, noted that effective leaders developed positive relationships among their colleagues. She emphasized that leadership fundamentally is enabling reciprocal processes and relationships among people to construct common meanings.

In turn, developing common meanings enables us to create subcultures within our organizations, such as schools and families. In short, as people interact and develop common meanings; they create shared norms and customs, shared expectations, which people develop in connection with social living (Linton 1955). We've just described how people create social systems and a culture. And this relates to chapter 3, "How to Make Sure We Stay Afloat . . . And How to Create a Healthy Subculture in the Process," which focuses on such organizational dynamics as roles and role expectations, social systems, and norms, in addition to creating a healthy subculture in the school.

The Role of Trust

Reflective Questions

1. What is the level of trust in your school?
2. Are you happy with it?

A major component of any effective leader's professional practice, and for a group to build an effective and positive subculture, is to develop *trust* among its members. Bryk and Schneider (2002) studied four hundred Chicago elementary schools for almost a decade, concluding that *relational trust* provides an absolutely essential underpinning in building effective educational communities.

Relational trust has two bases: social respect and personal regard. They discovered that relational trust strongly impacted schools' academic productivity and effectiveness and that such trust and accomplishment were considerably more likely to occur in small schools with a stable community. Obviously, this constitutes a rationale for decentralizing schools. But note that the trust is essential to generate greater academic achievement. Schools with low levels of relational trust had only a one in seven chance of becoming high in academic achievement, in contrast with one in two chances for those with high levels of trust.

More Leadership Themes

Isaacson (2004) discovered three crucial factors in teachers' perceptions of the theme of leadership:

- supporting teachers
- feeling appreciated
- providing a professional work environment

These indicators speak to a nonthreatening atmosphere that deals positively with interpersonal feelings. The atmosphere described by the teachers in their constructivist school was highly supportive, empowering, and provided support with ideas and suggestions. The indicator of feeling appreciated reeks with the fourth Maslowian (1954) level of Esteem, as well as his third step, Social Needs. Note that the third factor above (*providing a professional work environment*) speaks of respect, providing professional support in terms of facilities, supplies, providing time to work with teammates, and other professional needs.

The Rise of Small Learning Communities (SLCs) and Professional Learning Communities (PLCs)—and Process

Reflective Question

What are SLCs and PLCs and why are they so important?

By the third year of moving into a constructivist teaching model, the faculty was concerned enough for people newly entering the teaching profession to construct a model where the "newbies" were wrapped into PLCs. Every other Friday morning they were freed from the classroom to get in-serviced in areas they, the planning committee, and others deemed vital to their success.

Additionally, each selected an experienced mentor to help them through the trials and tribulations of their early experiences. The faculty was concerned to help them succeed, which is often not a factor in many schools where the staff is merely attempting to survive themselves. Chapters 11 and 12 consist of the three-year case study involving this school and deals with this much more fully.

A major piece of the reform of this school was to decentralize into SLCs, which also consisted of teams which made the school more personal since everyone knew everyone in the team or the small group called the SLC. Eventually, after teachers worked out many of their issues by developing more trust, respect, and acceptance of each other, they began to form PLCs to help each other grow professionally and personally.

Of particular interest to one and all was establishing the PLC to help new teachers become more skilled and more professional so that they would remain in the field, instead of being overwhelmed and leaving in despair. Thus, they did a lot of in-service work in the school, pulling in people with expertise in areas where they felt they had needs.

However, this points to the necessity of schools developing a plan and a process to stimulate professional growth among all of its personnel. As Clarence Darrow once noted, "The primary function of government is to strengthen the levels below."

This speaks to the issue of empowering people in the organization/ school. A very astute principal with whom I am presently working wants to "increase leadership density" ("Doc" H. Allen, Personal Communication, April 12, 2006). Isaacson discovered six dimensions of teachers as leaders, attesting to the success achieved in empowering teachers. All, 100 percent, reported feeling empowered in the school. Also, teachers felt that the principal's role was crucial in reforming the school, speaking to the larger issue of the principal's leadership role in organizational change. Empowerment was perceived since teachers were heavily involved in developing the change strategy and then implementing it.

Much written here speaks to the issue of *process*: Involving teachers in designing the change strategy, involving teachers fully in the entire process of change and then in reorganizing the school, involving teachers in establishing teams, SLCs and PLCs. These were the underlying underpinnings of empowering, resulting in such massive support for the reforms.

Additional Suggestions to Principals: Communication, Hierarchies, Power, Metaphors

Barnard is such an interesting source of nourishing ideas for the reform-minded executive. For example, if we take his notion of communicating as directly as possible to all the troops, it probably is wise to reduce the hierarchies cluttering up our organizations, which actively prevent communication and more personalized relationships. Hierarchies, although originally designed to organize more effectively, actually block.

Chapter 7, "Power and Its Uses—Sink or Swim" tries to state succinctly some insights into the constructive use of power for any leader and for the organization. A book such as this, dealing with reform, must dig into formulations of the nature of power, which probably should give some thought to its effective—and ineffective uses. People who do not think about it may lose power much more rapidly than they would like.

Chapter 4, "Metaphors and Images," chapter 5, "Five Parts of Organizations," and chapter 6, "Organizational Cycles," comprise food for thought for anyone in a leadership position.

Reflective Questions

1. What image(s) do you hold for the organization?
2. Is it one that you consciously want others to hold?
3. How do they affect your behavior?

These are serious questions for thoughtful leaders, who want to increase their effectiveness.

Another Reflective Question

How can we use the insights provided by Mintzberg's analysis of the impact of the pulls exerted by the five parts of the organization? See chapter 5.

I find Mintzberg's insights profound. His *Structuring of Organizations* is one of the few books I would have liked to have written (had I the knowledge to do it). It provides the person in a leadership position with the power to predict accurately what each of the five parts of the organization will do under many circumstances.

We've raised some insights afforded by the Tri-Partite Theory of Organizational Change and Succession above. Again, a theory such as this is quite useful for leaders in thinking about more effective function and in predicting the behavior of organizations, including their own.

Another interesting formulation regarding leadership was written by Robert Katz (1955), in which he teases out three skills of administrators. The first is technical knowledge of the field (how to teach effectively). The second is a human-relations dimension (the principal knows how to work effectively with people). The third is a conceptual dimension, in which the principal or leader is able to figure out where the district or society is going and is able to move the leader's own organization toward that direction.

Reflective Question

Don't you wish that General Motors, Ford, and others of our major financial organizations would have had such leaders at the top of the organization?

I also find that practicing the insights afforded by Maslow's Hierarchy of Needs (1954) is extremely useful in working with people, whether it be total schools, or classes, or administrators. As a superintendent, I tried to have coffee in my office. It calmed people down and made it much easier to talk productively. Meeting people's needs is probably a pretty good idea.

Chapter 4 presents a structure and strategy for anyone in a leadership position to *generate change as a routine*. It makes leading a lot easier. It's like having the Internet at one's disposal.

SUMMARY, EVEN SOME CONCLUSIONS AND IMPLICATIONS

This analysis took a deviant approach to leadership by looking at its dynamics, treating leadership as a social function and a social process. Several social functions of organizations and schools were provided together with their impact on leadership. Three role alternatives open for leaders to exert in their behavior were analyzed with the implication that to be effective, the more active second and third options were preferred. Leadership as a system of behavior was next treated, followed by the fundamental insights of Barnard regarding the leadership functions of executives. Analysis of the Tri-Partite Theory of Organizational Change and Succession provides insights into the careers of organizations as they usually career through a succession of three phases. Each phase is accompanied by a particular kind of leadership with a combination of the first two being considered a Synergist.

The necessity of establishing a philosophy to set directions for a school, as well as establishing positive relationships in which trust constitutes a major component, were discussed. A study of teachers' perceptions of leadership revealed three dimensions of leadership and six of teachers as leaders. The value of decentralizing into SLCs was pointed out. Also of value was developing PLCs to improve teachers' and administrators' skills and insights. Such crucial factors as involvement strategies to improve teacher buy-in and empowerment were provided, as was pointing to preceding chapters dealing with metaphors and images of organization, pulls on behavior from the five parts of the organization, and last, organizational cycles mentioned above.

Hopefully, these insights can assist us in becoming more effective in the daily hurly-burly of leadership.

IMPORTANT TERMS

Authority—see chapter 7 on power

Entropy—the generalization that all physical systems run downhill and decay. So do all organizations, including schools

Metaphor—a figure of speech in which a term is transferred from the object it ordinarily designates to an object it may designate only by implicit comparison or analogy (Mish 1988)

Professional Learning Community (PLC)—see chapter 12

Small Learning Community (SLC)—see chapters 11, 12, and 13

Social Function—various functions organizations provide to members of their society: governing, leadership, protection, socializing people into the culture and organizations, satisfying various needs

Social Process—people interacting with each other

III

STRATEGIES ON HOW TO GET THERE

All battles are won before they are fought.

—Sun Tsu

If you fail to plan, you plan to fail.

—Henry Cisneros, Secretary of Housing
and Urban Development (HUD)

9

Paddling into the Current

Top-Down Change Strategies, and This One—How to Pull It Off: Making Plans Work by Finessing Resistance

> There is no power for change greater than a community discovering what it cares about.
>
> —Margaret Wheatley

ORGANIZATIONAL CHANGE AND CHANGE STRATEGIES

Huge numbers of books have been written about organizational change, change strategies, and organizational development. Change strategies can be characterized in a variety of ways. One basic approach is that some are top-down (No Child Left Behind [NCLB], Florida's NCLB knock-off, the Florida Comprehensive Assessment Test [FCAT]), while others, such as the one used in the systems described in the following chapters, are bottom-up.

Top-down approaches usually generate a great deal of resentment and, consequently, resistance, as can be seen in the nationwide reaction to the pressures of NCLB. Bottom-up strategies generally involve people in the organizations, and if properly done, can generate cooperation and support, as well as effective reform. For the purpose of this book, we concentrate on the key elements of the Lewinian (1952) style strategy we used.

LEWIN'S CHANGE STRATEGY

Lewin's change strategy was born from his experiences in trying to change the behavior of mothers during World War II. Because of food shortages and new nutritional research-based findings, he was asked by the government to try to change people's food habits. Since we're a nation claiming to be individualists, he tried first to use lecture as an approach to change mothers' behavior. But that didn't work, since only 3 percent of women tried the foods most Americans did not use (sweetmeats, heart, kidneys). When he tried small-group discussion in which the women *publicly* agreed that they would change, 30 percent changed.

He tried these procedures again with orange juice and cod liver oil. "Lo and behold," the same results. Strangely, the mothers who made the public commitments increased their usage in the second and then the fourth weeks.

Lewin had discovered a fundamental effective change strategy, essentially the granddaddy of all change strategies.

Lewin's change strategy involves three steps.

1. The first is breaking the organization from the situation in which it sits, unfreezing, as Lewin termed it, from its norms and customs.
2. Step two is moving to a new level.
3. The third step is refreezing it into the new level, so that the new behavior "takes" and endures.

Lewin analyzed the processes he saw and came up with a tool called the *Force Field Analysis*. He thought any situation in an organization is roughly in a balance, which he called *"a quasi-stationary social equilibrium,"* meaning it was somewhat stable. That is, the opposing forces in the organization or situation were roughly balancing each other. Then he asked, what would break the semi-stable equilibrium from its quiescent state? Take smoking, which is difficult to change. How could it be changed?

Lewin analyzed the forces that keep one smoking (Driving Forces) and those in the semi-stationary equilibrium which might change it (Restraining Forces). Figure 9.1 is an example.

Instead of placing more pressure on the forces that oppose smoking, Lewin counseled *reducing* the strength of the forces that keep people smoking, the exact opposite of common sense.

Another example is an arms race. One nation gets a new weapon (a nuclear bomb, a trireme, a tank) and produces lots of them. Its chief antagonist nation immediately goes for the new weapon and once it gets it, produces lots of them.

How to deal with this?

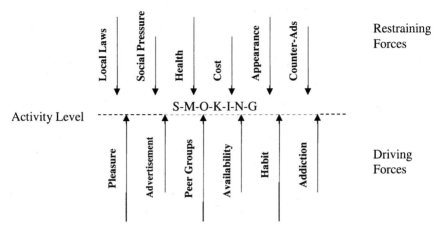

Figure 9.1.   A sample force field analysis of smoking behavior modified from Lewin

Reduce the number of bombs. The more bombs the one makes, the more the other makes. As for smoking, drinking coffee and smoking seem to be related. Reducing coffee drinking in many cases can lead to reduced smoking.

ANALYSIS OF THE STRATEGY USED: ANALYSIS OF THE DYNAMICS OF INDIVIDUALIZED ORGANIZATIONAL CHANGE

Viewing the figures of the strategy used in the succeeding chapters, it becomes evident that a great deal of care and thought went into designing the strategy so as to move the schools out of their quasi-stationary social equilibrium, that is, their state of inaction. Generally, this is best done by an outside consultant, who has no vested interest in the system. Next, of course, a Planning Task Force has to be established of key people from key social systems. If any social system is missed, problems will be generated inevitably.

The model developed as I was working with an elementary school which, of course, was experiencing enough difficulties to have the administration ask me to come in to figure out the problems and then to do something about them. First, I asked a Planning Committee of some key people about their *Concerns and Issues*. We spent two or three sessions on these and I wrote them down on large sheets of newsprint. Obviously, this was done very publicly. So many Concerns and Issues were offered that they became confusing, so I summarized them, and connected them with lines to their respective Concerns and Issues. These I labeled *Summaries*. But it seemed to me that we needed more than just the Summaries. So, I tried to figure out the *Underlying Themes* that underlay of each of the summarized Concerns and Issues, again with the Planning Committee, which we connected to the Summaries.

But figuring out the Underlying Themes was hardly sufficient to deal with the Concerns and Issues. What to do about resolving the Themes? We needed to figure out some *Potential Lines of Action* to deal with the Concerns and Issues and the Underlying Themes. As I was working on this with the Committee on the large sheets of newsprint, I suddenly stepped back and thought, "Holy Smoke, I've developed a bottom-up change strategy! And does it work!" (Shapiro 1994). Notice, we never talk about problems, since that tends to freeze people. Issues and concerns are the focus.

The model follows:

1. Meeting with the Planning Task Force and asking people what their Concerns and Issues are. Usually, this takes two or three meetings, normally after school, or during a half day. Since schools are complex organizations, people list sixty to eighty items, including lack of trust, jealousy, anger at individuals and social systems, concerns about discipline, kids lost in the school, administrators functioning or not functioning, guidance issues, a changing community leading to changing student attitudes and lack of parent participation, and many others. You know, normal Concerns and Issues.

2. Step two involves Summarizing the Concerns and Issues. No one can keep sixty items in mind, so we must summarize them to get a handle on the complexities, lining them up with the Concerns and Issues. Items included the teachers' social system fraying, student discipline a problem, teacher dissatisfaction, etc.

3. What are underlying Themes for the various Concerns and Issues. These might include trust-distrust, a changing community, a dysfunctional guidance department, the school too large to be personalized since people do not know each other, etc.

4. Potential Lines of Action get developed next. This takes a good deal of time, since the consultant and Task Force have to analyze the large amount of data that has been developed. Such optional ideas can include an in-service program to help teachers understand each other and their kids (and the administration), a major recognition program (shades of Maslow) since we all seem to need recognition, decentralizing into SLCs, a Classroom Teachers' Support Team, and other ideas to resolve the issues and concerns.

5. The *Underlying Rationale* for each of the steps ought to be developed, since it's useful to have a theoretical base for reforming situations and

schools. Examples might include helping faculty and administration understand and accept their kids better, understanding and accepting each other better, decentralizing to eliminate social distance and personalize the school as well as reducing student and teacher alienation, developing an activities program for kids, etc.

6. The last step consists of Major Outcomes, such as decentralizing into SLCs or teams, an in-service program on understanding each other and the kids, a conflict management program (since often elementary teachers do not confront each other readily to resolve issues), trust-building exercises, etc.

Well, that's it.

SUMMARY

We have presented a bottom-up change strategy that seems to work like a charm as a major approach to reforming schools. The next chapters include a junior high turned into a model middle school, two chapters (before and after) of an elementary school that became the model in a very large district so that teachers begged to teach there, and an inner-city high school that shed its negative image, and became quite effective.

IMPORTANT TERMS

Freezing—making sure that the changes become embedded into the organization's practices

Force Field Analysis—analyzing the forces in a social system that keep it in balance to change it

Quasi-stationary Social Equilibrium—the forces in a social system that keep it from changing

Unfreezing—changing a social practice or practices and moving to a new series of practices

IV

THREE CASE STUDIES TO DEMONSTRATE HOW TO PULL OFF IMPROVING SCHOOLS BY DECENTRALIZING

You must love those you lead before you can be an effective leader. You certainly can command without that sense of commitment, but you cannot lead without it. And without leadership, command is a hollow experience, a vacuum often filled with mistrust and arrogance.

—Four-Star General Erik K. Shinseki, United States Army Chief of Staff

10

Example 1: Beliefs, Myths, and Realities: Decentralizing a Rogue Junior High into a Model Middle School (Despite the Riptides)

There is nothing more difficult to take in hand, more perilous to conduct, or more uncertain in its success, than to take the lead in the introduction of a new order of things.

—Niccolo Machiavelli, *The Prince*

Using a bottom-up change strategy, which I called *Analysis of the Dynamics of Organizational Change* (Burley and Shapiro 1994; Shapiro 1994; Shapiro, Benjamin, and Hunt 1995)—a highly individualized diagnostic, analytic, and implementation strategy—we decentralized a rogue junior high school, in the process facilitating its becoming a model middle school for a district. Oddly, the year after this school started changing, the other junior highs also shifted into a decentralized, much more personal approach. Here's how it was pulled off.

BEGINNINGS

Reflective Questions

1. What do we mean by *Analysis of the Dynamics of Organizational Change, an Organizational Mapping approach*?
2. Why is it an individualized diagnostic, analytical, and implementing change strategy?

Read on.

So, what do you do when a colleague you like, essentially a very gentle and dedicated man, asks if you would like to work with a school that seemed to be having some problems?

Intrigued, you respond by saying, "Sure."

So, off Wade Burley and I went to chat with an assistant superintendent who had his head on straight and a supervisor who had taught in the school. After the normal schmoozing (read, chitchat), the pair seemed to accept me (I hoped), and started to describe the school, a junior high that seemed alienated from the district, and was not only quite distrustful of, but also even hostile to the central office.

All too often, the administrators didn't bother to show up for key meetings for principals, and about as frequently ignored central office policies that all the other schools followed, such as the policy against suspending and then sending a junior high kid to walk home across four miles of major thoroughfares and railroad tracks. They also made numerous derogatory comments about the central office administration rather publicly, and the school's teachers, even in interviews for promotions, made disparaging comments about central office people to their faces, which the latter found quite disquieting.

CALLING IN THE CAVALRY

Rather than punishing the school, the administrators were concerned enough to ask for help. When I indicated that they seemed to have a rogue school on their hands they agreed, although Wade almost fell off his chair at the comment.

Wade and I agreed on the rudiments of a change strategy in our conversations, the first step being to have lunch with the principal, who turned out to be an easygoing man committed to his students and faculty, and we hoped he would accept us. If so (and he did), we would urge him to establish a planning committee of high prestige teachers, at least one counselor, the assistant principal, and other key people to deal with some of the issues and concerns the teachers and administration perceived they faced. He agreed, and did so. We set up a date for the committee to meet right after school.

COMMONLY USED CHANGE
STRATEGIES VERSUS EFFECTIVE ONES

The Favorite *Belief* and *Myth*: The Top-Down Quick Fix

Now for a few not-so-random thoughts about making effective changes in schools. We Americans go for a quick fix.

Reflective Questions

1. Do you want an example?
2. What is the best way to eliminate gangs?
3. Or, how does a company such as Chrysler reform itself?
4. Or (same issue) what is the best and quickest way to make sure that all the schools in a district or districts in a state or districts in the country become reformed fast—real fast?

Use an overall strategy from the top, usually with a lot of coercion.
Does it work?
Of course not.
About dealing with gangs effectively? First, we have to find out why people join and stay in them. They have very good reasons for their action. And then, we have to grasp the essential nature of any human system (and gangs are systems). That's why we're generally quite ineffective in dealing with them. See chapter 3, "How to Make Sure We Stay Afloat . . .," for the dynamics involved in groups/social systems.

It takes enormous effort, time, resources, commitment, etc., to reform just one company, or a single school. (For example, look how long it was taking Daimler to reform Chrysler—and they gave up). So far, we and they are not too successful in such reform enterprises.

(Surprise!)

And Now, for *Reality*

As for schools, each school and district is an exceedingly complex entity that *resists change*. Sarason's (1971) book title, *The Culture of the School and the Problem of Change*, states it all. His reissued book, *Revisiting the Culture of the School and the Problem of Social Change* (1996) (note the addition of the word, *"Social"*), recertifies his original thesis.

All human systems such as schools develop a *culture*, that is, a set of patterns of common understandings, customs, and practices (norms), feelings, and beliefs that gradually develop as people live with each other. Another quick description is that a culture consists of patterns of shared, learned behavior (Linton 1955). Your family develops a culture, so does your school, so does any store, and every system. And they differ (for instance, compare the culture of a nursery school with that of the U.S. Marines. Marines usually don't have cookies and naps).

Most school reform attempts become top-down strategies, since people design them based on often somewhat simplistic beliefs on how to change complex systems, and generally consist of a one-size-fits-all strategy. The Annie E. Casey Foundation approached schools with this model, as did the Coalition of Essential Schools, and so do virtually all states (while talking from the other side of their mouths about site-based management or decision making). The shelf life of most reform efforts, as a result, is usually relatively short—and then the next panacea arrives to fix everything and bring back the wonderful years of yore (that never existed).

Fortunately, I have been able to work with a lot of schools and districts to develop effective changes—not the easiest task—as we sort of implied. In the course of working with several schools previously, a change strategy fell out. That is, a pattern or a model emerged. Wade and I talked about this model and how to apply it to the junior high.

THE CHANGE STRATEGY IN ACTION: MAPPING THE SCHOOL TO MOVE IT INTO A MODEL MIDDLE SCHOOL

The model is essentially a highly individualized diagnostic, analytic, and implementation change strategy. That is, it diagnoses (maps) each school on its own merits, assuming little, if anything. As a result, since each school is quite different from others (although they all have commonalities), each reform or change effort must take these differences into account and then develop different courses or lines of action to make effective changes. A one-size-fits-all strategy not only doesn't cut it, it also misleads reform efforts significantly.

Obviously, first we had to make certain that the central office, including the superintendent, supported these intentions. They did. He did. We also consulted with the Teachers' Association. They were highly supportive, and wondered at first whether a partially grey-haired university prof could relate effectively with hard-pressed teachers on the firing line. I told them that I appreciated their straightforward honesty.

Reflective Question

How was the change strategy applied to this junior high? See table 10.1.

CONCERNS, ISSUES

Reflective Question

What Concerns and Issues did the people perceive?

Note we didn't say *problems*. Mention problems—people freeze.

For our first meeting we brought some refreshments (grapes, apples, cantaloupe, cookies) so that people, tired from a full day, could relax, grab a bite, socialize a bit, watch us surreptitiously, and then look at some of their

Table 10.1. Analysis of Dynamics of Change

Issues/Questions	Summary/Conclusions	Potential Lines of Action/Initiative
Socioeconomic changes in community From single home to duplexes From parents to single parents Reduced intramural participation Reduced parents' participation	Changing student values attitudes Value of education Not doing homework Impact on teachers Reduced standards	Major intramural program Major recognition program Major involvement of parents Volunteers in school Fund raisers Administration, faculty involved In-service programs to understand students
Impact on teachers Feelings of high stress High frustration Morale collapsing "Family" feeling collapsing Considering leaving school	Social organization holding school together, but fraying Key teacher social systems upset, publicly considering leaving	Develop grade level administrative teams Develop teacher teams
Hopelessness	Need sense of hope	Develop plan with purpose Form three committees to reorganize Planning Guidance Classroom management support team
Passive, laissez faire Administration not functioning One of two deans not functioning Guidance dysfunctional Administrative clock-watching Spreading to teachers, students	Administration, deans, guidance dysfunctional Not cooperating Not proactive Limited work ethic affecting teachers, students Teachers angry to students for this	Proactive leadership to form and support Planning and guidance committees

(*continued*)

Table 10.1. (*Continued*)

Issues/Questions	Summary/Conclusions	Potential Lines of Action/Initiative
Junior high school departmental organization dysfunctional	Formal organization blocks effective action Isolates teachers Teachers with same students do not see each other Teachers disorganized	Formal organization must change to facilitate cooperation Form teacher teams, work in small decentralized units with same students Form grade level administrative teams
Departmental organization	Little accountability	Grade-level teams for administrators, teachers
Norms (attitudes, practices, behavior)	Culture dysfunctional Norms must change	Establish new norms with above changes

Rationale for Action	Underlying Themes	Major Outcomes
Develop sense of belonging for all Sense that teachers care, that parents care Sense of pride Teach parenting skills Faculty, administration understand, accept students Involve community	Changing community changes students' attitudes Decreasing respect for teachers, education Teachers increasingly alienated from parents, students, each other, administration, guidance, central office	Major intramural programs Major recognition program for all Major parent involvement program, with staff development In-service program on nature of students
Decentralize Work/cooperate in small units Makes all visible/accountable Personalizes Increases ownership, morale Increases sense of belonging	Teachers, control over professional life decreased Feel powerless School sliding downhill	Grade-level administrative teams in place Teacher teams in operation
Teachers involved in reorganization increases ownership Empowerment Support groups	Loss of morale, hope, positive attitude toward work, purpose	Long-range plan developed Reorganization support team functioning Sense of hope Strong teacher ownership of plan and support of reorganization support team

Rationale for Action	Underlying Themes	Major Outcomes
Develop support by all reference (administration, deans, guidance, faculty, students, community, central office)	Passive, laissez faire administration functioning poorly No accountability	Administration strongly supports plan, reorganization support team, process Accountability clear, visible
Decentralizing facilitates Personalizing Empowerment Greater responsibility Accountability—all visible Cooperation Interdependent operation	Relationship between form and function Organization dysfunctional— prohibits teachers with same students teams Centralized/decentralized Central office indifferent	Formal organization changed from a junior high school to a middle school Grade-level administrative Teacher teams with block of students Implementing teacher as advisor program
All organizational components become visible—thus, accountable	Administrators, deans, guidance not accountable	Accountability
Decentralization increases students', teachers' cooperation, responsibility	Norms need to support changes, work ethic, cooperation, responsible professional behavior, self-esteem, recognition for all, repersonalizing to a family	Cultural norms, beliefs, practices changed

concerns and issues. First, of course, people sized us up; the principal made introductions and some started to accept us.

Fortunately, Wade had been working with the district for fifteen years or so as the university rep with their Teacher Education Center Planning Council, so was well known and accepted. So he kindly dragged me along on his coattails. But trust and acceptance take time.

I put up 24" by 36" chart paper on the wall and asked folks what their major concerns were, and wrote them down with colored markers. About two sessions every other week after school were used to get these perceptions and feelings out.

Here's a summary:

The teachers were most concerned about *socioeconomic* changes in the community, which were causing their students to *value education* less. Working mothers were less able to take their kids home from the *intramurals*, which the faculty really valued, so that program collapsed.

Teachers, as a consequence, felt highly stressed, and perceived their *morale* declining.

Indeed, people talked about transferring—and one high-status person did transfer, to the great shock of the faculty, most of whom had been there almost two decades.

Their *work ethic* suffered, so people left school as early as they could.

Their sense of *hopelessness* zoomed up.

The administration and guidance counselors were really *not functioning*.

The *junior high school structure* of isolated departments was preventing faculty from communicating with each other and dealing effectively with the kids.

See the first column in table 10.1, *Issues, Questions*, which displays this information.

It should be noted that all these points were then printed on paper with copies being given to everyone, including office staff and custodians, to make sure that we set up a system of communication with and for everyone. That way you get buy-in.

Reflective Question

OK, what's the next step?

SUMMARY, CONCLUSIONS

We next summarized these perceptions on the paper, which are the basis for the second column in table 10.1, *Summary/Conclusions*.

Since students' *value for education* was reduced, homework was not being done.

Teachers did not want to reduce their *standards*, and mourned the loss of their *intramural program*—so, they became annoyed and angry with the kids.

The *social structure* holding the school together was fraying, leading to key teacher social systems becoming very upset, and publicly contemplating leaving.

Hope is the gasoline of any social system—it was evaporating.

The *administration and guidance were dysfunctional*, too passive.

The formal *departmental structure* was blocking effective action, isolating teachers since only people from the same department could interact with each other, which prevented faculty teaching the same kids, but in different subjects, from communicating.

The *culture was dysfunctional*; norms must change.

Table 10.1 diagrams Concerns and Issues, and the next related column, Summary/Conclusions.

After this, a faculty meeting was called, at which we went thoroughly through the findings and conclusions. One faculty member noted that all the indicators were downhill, which I corroborated. The assistant principal then noted that we had better do something. (Note that Lewin's [1952] first step of change, unfreezing to move to a new level, was accomplished. Our task was to move the school to a new level and then refreeze it into a new pattern).

UNDERLYING THEMES

The next stage was to analyze the Themes that underlay the Concerns and Issues:

A *changing community* led to *changed student attitudes and values.*

These were reflected in reduced *value for education.*

In turn the teachers became increasingly *alienated* from the community, parents, kids, each other, the administration—and angry with the kids.

Teachers' control over their professional life became reduced, so they felt *powerless.*

The school's sense of *hope* slipped, as did *morale and esprit de corps.*

The *passive, laissez faire administration and guidance* were functioning poorly.

The *departmental structure* was dysfunctional, prohibiting teachers with the same kids from working together, leading to the kids being organized and teachers not.

The administration and deans were *not accountable* with this departmental structure.

Norms needed to support work changes, cooperation, work ethic, *recognition* for everyone from the custodians to the students to the teachers to the administration (Maslow 1954).

Table 10.1 reveals the progression from Concerns/Issues, to Summary/ Conclusions, to the third column, Underlying Themes (of Concerns and Issues).

POTENTIAL LINES OF ACTION/INITIATIVES

To get maximum feedback and communication with the entire staff, we drew up an eighteen-item questionnaire and asked teachers to list their five greatest concerns.

The four highest were:

1. The present operational role of *guidance and counseling*
2. *Unified, consistent procedures* for handling student *discipline* by faculty
3. *Student attitudes toward education*
4. Total staff *morale* (faculty, administration, others)

The next step in this individualized change strategy was to look at possible Lines of Action to change norms, practices, structure, and processes. This we did:

Since the faculty highly valued their *intramural program, resuscitate it.*

Since everyone needs recognition (shades of Maslow), institute a major *recognition* program. To do this, place photos of everyone doing something significant on the glass by the front office, an area that everyone passes into, around, and out of the school.

Develop major programs to *involve parents and involve teachers and administrators.*

Institute *in-service programs* to understand kids and community better.

Reorganize the school *into grade-level administrative teams and teacher teams.*

Develop a *plan* with a purpose.

Therefore, form *three committees* to reorganize the school.

- *Planning* Committee.
- *Guidance* Committee.
- *Classroom-Management Support Team* to help new teachers with discipline problems, for utilization by the principal at his discretion.

    Leadership has to become more *proactive and support* these initiatives.

    The formal junior-high departmental structure must change to facilitate cooperation among teachers by forming *grade-level administrative teams* and by beginning to form *teacher teams,* thus *decentralizing* the school into *SLCs.*

    Establish *new norms* in line with the above changes.

You will note that table 10.1 presents these and their relationships to Concerns/Issues, next a Summary/Conclusions of these Concerns/Issues, then Underlying Themes, and then in column four, Potential Lines of Action/Initiatives.

RATIONALE FOR ACTIONS

Reflective Question

Why search for rationales?

You're much better off if you can base actions on clear research. It just so happens that each of these changes obviously is based on theoretical and pragmatic grounds. The following digs at them.

Develop a sense of *belonging* for all. Humans are social animals and need this. Maslow (1954) is a basis for this. This demonstrates to kids that parents and teachers care.

Teach *parenting* skills.

Involve community.

Demonstrate that teachers and administration *understand and accept* kids and community.

Decentralize into teams.

Increases sense of belonging, ownership, morale, personalizes (you know everyone on your team).

All structural components become visible, thereby making everyone visible and accountable.

Empowers, fosters cooperation, interdependence.

Involve teachers, administration, guidance, community, central office in reorganizing, which increases ownership and empowerment.

Establish support groups.

In table 10.1, the Rationale, in column five, is presented for Potential Lines of Action.

MAJOR OUTCOMES

The last column in table 10.1 presents Outcomes. While this may appear a bit mechanical, it was anything but that. As the above were shared with faculty, a planning and decision-making workshop was held before the close of school. At that time, the following was decided upon for implementation. Note that Lewin's second step in his granddaddy of change models was achieved, namely, moving to a new level—that is, implementing changes—and then freezing them into daily practice.

Note also that expectations, norms, and roles changed:

A major *intramural* program was instituted.

A major *recognition* program was developed and instituted, placing color photos of anyone who did anything significant on the office glass wall. People crowded around it.

A major *parent involvement* program, with staff development, and an *in-service* program on the nature of the students was implemented. Teachers gave up their evening basketball session to staff this, since earlier teacher attendance at parent meetings was erratic (a euphemism, to be sure). A fundraiser was implemented and $14,000 was raised to everyone's astonishment and delight. Parents were welcomed as a volunteer program surfaced.

The school was *restructured into three houses* each consisting of a different grade level with its own *administrative team* (dean/administrator, counselor, secretary/clerk).

Two volunteer *teacher teams* at the sixth-grade level were agreed upon and implemented, leaving people not ready to move into that model to teach traditionally.

A *long-range plan* was developed, including:

- A *Reorganization Support Team* from the Planning and Guidance Teams.
- A *Classroom-Management Support Team* of status teachers to help anyone needing it, as assigned by the principal.

Our repeat of the survey used the preceding year, which was given toward the end of the following school year, indicated:

A sense of *hope* had developed.

Teachers felt strong *ownership* of the plan and supported the Reorganization Support Team.

Amazingly, all eighteen questions regarding satisfaction showed improvement, some indicating considerable improvement.

And for the two following years, we were astonished to find that satisfaction increased on all eighteen questions.

The administration, of both the school and the central office, strongly supported the plan, the Reorganization Support Team, and the process. The central administration added a counselor to the school to facilitate the plan.

Accountability, murky before, now was clear; everyone was very visible.

The following year the sixth-grade team increased its teams from two to three, involving all teachers. The seventh and eighth grades each developed a volunteer team. By the succeeding third year, all teachers in these three grades worked on teams. Much to our surprise, the special teachers (art, physical education, industrial arts, special education) also joined these teams:

> Key *social systems* of the school served on the Reorganization Support Team, indicating intense support. Regular meetings of this team saw virtually 100 percent attendance at all times. One member refused coaching assignments to retain membership on this team.
>
> *In-service* training was provided to teams and to grade-level administrative teams to function better, the latter group to supervise more effectively.
>
> Clerks/secretaries contributed considerably by meeting regularly to improve *their* function. Their minutes, as well as the minutes of every meeting of the Reorganization Support Team, were provided to everyone, making sure that the system of communication worked.

MORE RESULTS—REALLY, AN EPILOGUE

The central office administrator who initiated our work called the school "one of the most improved schools in the county."

Three of the four highest priorities for the faculty changed radically by the end of the second year:

> #1 to 15th: "The present operational role of guidance and counseling."
> #2 to 5th: "Unified, consistent procedures for handling student discipline."
> #3 to #3: "Student attitude toward education."
> #4 to #1: "Staff morale."

Now they could work on morale and student attitudes. The others had been cleaned up.

Attitudes toward students changed. With decentralization and teaming into SLCs, many fewer kids were sent to the office, and less anger was being expressed toward kids.

With the implementation of teams, everyone gets to know each other, a family feeling develops, people get to care for each other, and teams "take care of our own." Teachers become advocates for "their" kids since they were all in the same SLC.

Student surveys indicated more positive attitudes also.

An ineffective junior high became an effective decentralized, team-taught, SLC-based middle school.

At an annual party celebrating the end of the second year of implementation, at least seventeen people told us that it was the most successful year in education they had ever had professionally.

Here are anonymous comments at the end of the second year of implementation, when we asked "How have things changed at the school over the past three years?"

The office is working beautifully and people seem to know what their roles are and generally are comfortable with them. Because of more effective in-service, there is less negativism and more willingness to try new ideas. Most of us feel we are having a positive effect on our students.

Teaming is working well so far.

There has been a positive attitude at (the) top . . . accountability . . . visibility of all staff (members) have changed.

I think the front office alignment has worked out beautifully. Grade level adms. (administrators), counselors, and staff have worked well.

We have been exposed to new ideas and ways of doing things. Staff has had more opportunities to interact in a variety of settings and in some cases "forced" to work together. I think this has been beneficial in sharing needs, concerns, and frustrations among staff members rather than in just departments. We have all been looking for an easy fix for other problems; but we are learning that with assistance and input of other experts, we have the answers to the future of our kids if we will patiently and cooperatively put it all together. We are not there yet; but we have made some huge strides.

Note

By the end of the third year all junior high schools in the district had used this model to become middle schools. When I mentioned in passing that the central administration considered this school the district's model middle school, the faculty members were amazed. Several thought for some time that I was putting them on.

Several years later, one of my students who joined the faculty after all this had occurred, mentioned to the Director of Guidance services that he was taking a course with me. The Director told him that working in the school after the changes had been made were the best years of her professional life. She could function as a professional.

QUESTIONS

1. Is there another change strategy you might think about using to deal with these complex issues?
   A. Lewin's Force Field Analysis approach? If so, how would you proceed?
2. What do you think of the change strategy we used, which we called *Analysis of Dynamics of Organizational Change*?
   A. What are its strengths? Its focus?
   B. Its weaknesses? What does it miss?
   C. How could it be improved? [If you can figure out a way to do this, please contact me.]
3. What alternative strategies would you use to get into the school?
   A. To become established/accepted?
   B. What other underlying themes do you perceive?
   C. What alternative lines of action could you develop to improve the school?
   D. And, what are the rationales underlying these lines of action?
   E. What other outcomes might you predict might occur?
4. Why do you think that the other junior highs changed without any help into middle schools, essentially using the same model we developed?
   A. What advantages do you see over the old junior high model?
   B. What advantages do you think they perceived?
5. What other questions would you ask?

IMPORTANT TERMS

Analysis of Dynamics of Organizational Change—a change strategy based on getting information from the people on all levels of the organization. A bottom-up change strategy.
Organizational Mapping—see above

11

Example 2: Moving a Large Elementary School into a Decentralized Constructivist Model (and the Scores Jumped Up)

> To accomplish great things,
> we must not only act,
> but also dream,
> not only plan,
> but also believe.
>
> —Anatole France

> Help me—I'm drowning!
>
> —Lynne Menard, assistant principal and Berbecker Fellowship Fellow,
> comparing teachers' statements in chapters 11 and 12

Reflective Question

What do you do when a high-energy elementary principal, starting her doctorate, asks you to help resolve conflict between a group of excellent teachers, who had come from a widely known and celebrated school with an equally competent veteran faculty? She also wanted to move the entire large school toward constructivist instruction.

Note: The next chapter, chapter 12, presents the school three years later, after it became constructivist. A subsequent study two years later determined if the school retained its constructivist philosophy and teaching practices.

It did.

Both these comments got my attention.
Better have a good change strategy in your hand (or your head).
Fortunately, I did.

ORGANIZING FOR CHANGE

Outside Facilitator

The principal noted that to focus on needed priorities, it was necessary to involve someone in organizational development to facilitate discussion and analysis, particularly when issues and problems are complex. Bringing in outside facilitators is supported by literature (Beckhard 1969; Mintzberg 1994).

Sitting down with the principal was a first step, particularly focusing on Concerns and Issues people felt. First, of course, we chatted about each other.

The Principal

She was one of a declining number of female principals in a Western state, migrated for a change of scenery, served several years as a teacher to become certified in a new state, did it with a sense of humor, underwent a year as an intern principal, and finally, became a principal. When the district decided to build a new school, she was chosen as principal.

One reason was the district's confidence in her. Teachers joked that the district left her alone, because she obviously was so competent. Being unassuming, she thought that was amusing. People knew that she was not afraid to take risks (for example, moving in mid-career to a new state where she first had to become a teacher to qualify as a principal, an administrative intern next).

A Major (and Unexpected) Source of Conflict

One source of conflict was that a group of new people, all excellent teachers, suffered huge disappointments in their former school as its widely heralded mission for which they were recruited nationally, and to which they were deeply committed, changed rapidly into a traditional school.

Consequently, feeling betrayed, they came into this school feeling defensive, "coming in with their guns blazing." As a result, perfectly normal organizational processes immediately surfaced, such as issues of trust/distrust, we/they (acceptance/rejection), and defensiveness.

When groups enter organizations, conflict often occurs based upon perceived differences between old and new groups for a variety of predictable reasons. Experienced people often are hired to enrich the organization; however, with experience comes their own set of norms, which can be perceived as threatening to the established subculture. Because these folks entered as a group rather than individuals who could be more easily assimilated, their impact was greater.

Resolving This

The change strategy, reflection, and dialogue helped people realize that apparent conflicts in norms and beliefs did not exist. The new folks referred to methods of instruction by different labels, which led to a build-up of resentment since the "newbies" were perceived as trying to take over. Once teams discussed specific reading strategies, rather than specific labels, resistance regarding instructional differences vanished. It was still necessary to build trust before discussions as near to the heart of teachers as instructional strategies could become productive.

The School—Briefly

Southwood Elementary school, with over nine hundred students, was in its third year, with a growing community mostly of people living in homes, with increasing immigrants from a variety of cultures and nations. Socio-economically, it was middle and working class.

USING THE ANALYSIS OF DYNAMICS OF ORGANIZATIONAL CHANGE: A DIAGNOSING, ANALYZING, PLANNING, AND IMPLEMENTING STRATEGY

This Analysis of Dynamics of Organizational Change (Burley and Shapiro 1994; Shapiro 1994; Shapiro, Benjamin and Hunt, 1995; Shapiro 2000) model and planning process flowed out of work with several schools and a hospital. Actually, as I was working with faculty and administration in each school, trying to grasp the complexities of two schools, the model fell out. I stepped back from the chart paper sheets on the wall, and thought, "Holy smoke, I've come up with a bottom-up change model!" Obviously, it is a constructivist change strategy since it works from teachers' input. It is also Lewinian (1952) since it breaks the system out of present practices, moves to a new level, and refreezes the new norms/culture.

An Individualized Constructivist Change Model

It's considerably beyond a simple change strategy, enabling one first to *diagnose and analyze* any organization's Concerns and Issues, next to

Summarize them, and then to dig away at Underlying Themes to get a sense of what factors and dynamics underlie the Concerns and Issues. The fourth step is to develop Potential Lines of Action, (a Plan) to deal with them, next to look at Underlying Rationales for each Line of Action, and last to *analyze* Consequences and Outcomes of implementing the plan as it evolves. See figure 11.1.

In short, it is a highly *individualized* constructivist bottom-up change strategy in stark contrast with most attempts that try to change organizations top-down, the usual strategy for most national foundations' efforts, our own national efforts, such as Goals 2000 and NCLB, and many state change strategies, such as Florida's Comprehensive Assessment Test (FCAT). (See Hunt, Benjamin, and Shapiro 2004, *What Florida Teachers Say About the FCAT*, for teachers' perceptions about a change strategy shoved down their throats.)

All, of course, are fatally flawed, since the outsiders use one change strategy to try to force very complex organizations to move in a direction they've decided upon. And the inhabitants exhibit resistance, at which they are very good!

States, which use tests to force districts to move in directions they unilaterally and politically decide upon, generally find the teaching profession vigorously opposed to such coercion. Individual schools and districts that use top-down change strategies generally have them implemented by only a few true believers, who usually leave after a short while because they get sick and tired of the slings and arrows aimed their way. The Annie E. Casey Foundation's attempt reveals this (Wehlage, Smith, and Lipman 1992), as does the Coalition of Essential Schools (Muncey and McQuillan 1993).

This diagnostic, analytic, implementation, and change strategy is a process of *"Organizational Mapping,"* uncovering processes organizations generate in their functioning. The resultant figure I titled "The Analysis of Dynamics of Organizational Change" (Burley and Shapiro 1994; Shapiro 1994; Shapiro, Benjamin, and Hunt 1995; Shapiro 2000).

In addition, modeling constructivist thinking requires focusing on higher cognitive levels, such as dealing with Concerns and Issues, analyzing underlying Themes, constructing a Plan to deal with Concerns and Issues, analyzing Outcomes, and finally, evaluating them.

Reflective Question

How similar is this to the process of getting accepted by people with whom we are working?

- The first stage, informal, of course, is to get people's confidence, particularly the confidence of those able to make decisions. Otherwise, you're out on your ear.

- The next step, still informal, is to get a representative *Planning Committee* of key people who are trusted and represent all shades of opinions and feelings. (If you stack the deck by making it unrepresentative, you will destroy its and your credibility.)
- Next, we have to get at underlying Concerns and Issues people perceive. This takes time, and cannot be rushed, otherwise we will miss something crucial. These Concerns and Issues have to be written on large sheets of chart paper for the Planning Committee to see. Then, they must be reduced to fit on a 8½" × 11" paper, and sent to *everyone* (and I mean, everyone—or the uninformed will get upset, suspicious, and harm the effort), teachers, PTA, and office staff, ensuring immediate effective *communication* (shades of Barnard) to one and all. No one can be left out—or they will feel—and be, left out. When it comes time to need their support—they won't be there!
- The succeeding step is to Summarize those many Concerns and Issues.
- Next, we analyze Underlying Themes, which unify the inquiry and also winnow down insights into a few handleable factors that underlie peoples' concerns.
- Next, we try to figure out Potential Lines of Action/Initiatives to take action to resolve Concerns and Issues and Themes.
- We then work at figuring out underlying Rationales for each Potential Line of Action/Initiative.
- The last step is to evaluate Outcomes, or Consequences of each Line of Action. See figure 11.1.

This is really simpler than one might think (if people develop confidence in you). It just takes time. It is useful to listen very carefully to everything said to pull off an accurate and thoughtful diagnosis. Listening for side (and snide) comments and watching for body language is vital.

FIRST, A PLANNING COMMITTEE

Substantial, respected people had to be selected from all kindergarten through fifth grades. The group had to have representatives from newer teachers recruited. Fortunately, the curriculum specialist came from that school, was active in recruiting them, and was trusted and perceived as a highly competent, caring woman of integrity, committed to the school and staff. She and one teacher from the "contributing" school served.

When, at about noon, I walked into the planning committee near the main office area, people were there, and the principal arranged for sandwiches, potato chips, fruit, some candy, and lots of markers. I had lugged in my 24" by 36" chart paper, along with tape and markers. People were very friendly, all of us covertly sizing each other up, as we ate and socialized.

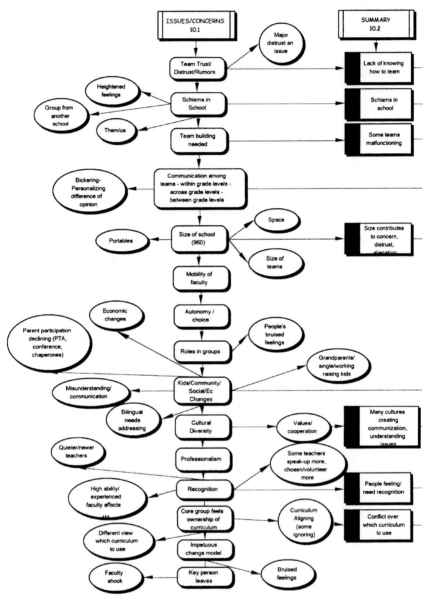

Figure 11.1. Analysis of Dynamics of Organizational Change (*continued on next page*)

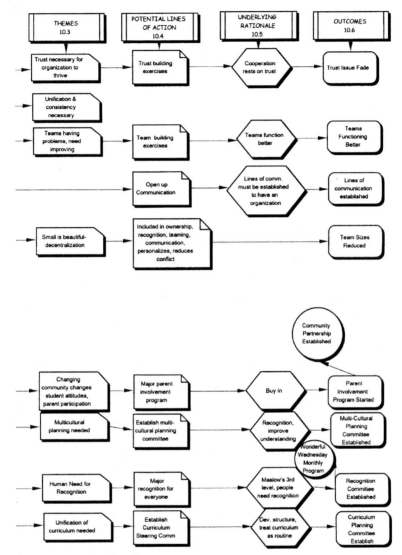

Figure 11.1. (*Continued*)

Introductions

We settled down and everyone introduced themselves, some personal stuff was said, some professional. The principal introduced me, mostly stressing very briefly my work as a teacher and administrator, working with a variety of schools. We had a representative from every grade, the principal, the curriculum assistant, a technology/graphics specialist who took notes, and me.

The graphics expert, who was really talented, was able to transfer my printing on the long, taped-up sheets of chart paper into figures that made my illegible scratchings legible. She was able to construct graphic figures, a terrific help in visualizing issues, as can be seen in figure 11.1. She did this on the spot, so that minutes were available immediately at the end of each meeting (meeting Barnard's [1938] admonition of establishing direct lines of communication as one of his three indispensable elements of executive function [establishing a common purpose, and a system of cooperation are the other two]).

PURPOSES

The principal explained purposes, one of which was to deal with the conflict, another to think about moving toward vertical teaming, and anything else we could come up with to improve the school and learning for kids. This was a pretty wide-open agenda, so people knew their input was crucial.

We then moved to using the *"Organizational Mapping"* model to develop insights.

DEVELOP EVERYONE'S CONCERNS AND ISSUES

Many people working with organizations tend to ask people about *problems* they face. Note that we did *not* talk about problems, rather, Concerns and Issues. Why? Talking about problems often blocks discussion, since people may start complaining, rather than analyzing their issues and concerns.

People usually respond to this relatively forthrightly, openly (so, I felt they were beginning to trust me).

The first Concern/Issue raised was that of *team trust/distrust/rumors*. People felt that distrust was a major issue. The group from the other school was quite taken aback by this perception of them/us, by perceptions of *schisms*. (Not to worry, though; by October of the following semester, this had disappeared from the radar and didn't register as a blip.)

There I was, up on a step stool, marking Concerns and Issues on long sheets of chart paper, all taped together.

As figure 11.1 indicates, a number of Concerns and Issues surfaced, which are summarized in the succeeding column, Summarizing Concerns and Issues.

- Team trust/distrust rumors swirling about, creating schisms in the school, generating distrust, them/us feelings
- Team building needed to improve functioning.
- Curriculum a concern:
  - in terms of aligning
  - differing views about what curriculum to use
  - some ignoring alignments
- Communication a major concern:
  - communication with administration
  - among teams, within, across, among grade levels
- Bickering, struggles for control, differences of opinion personalized, leading to hurt feelings
- Size of school an important issue in functioning of organizations
- Size of teams is an issue, some being comprised of eight teachers; to which I responded that eight was too large to communicate and to work together. Thelen (1949) noted the maximum number of roles available in work groups appeared to be seven. Once you had more than seven, quieter, less assertive persons will be squeezed out, participating less.
- In its first three years, the school grew, causing staff mobility.
- Faculty felt their autonomy (synonymous with professionalism) was honored.
- Social and economic changes occurring in the community:
  - parent participation declining
  - PTA conferences not as well attended
  - fewer chaperones available for field trips
  - more grandparents raising kids
  - more single moms working and raising kids
- An influx of immigrants, some doubling and tripling families living in houses:
  - greater cultural diversity occurring, leading to misunderstanding
  - more bilingual needs for students, nineteen languages spoken (three years later, fifty-four)
  - some kids not motivated
- I asked how satisfied people felt with recognition they were getting.
- A key person left (the charismatic second-in-command) in the previous mid-year:
  - causing great sense of loss, purpose, hurt feelings, morale

- The group from the other school coming on board:
  - leading to little trust
  - them/us feelings
- Gifted program needs addressing:
  - "It doesn't appear that much has been going on this year."

We impatient Americans might ask: what kinds of *actions* can be taken to deal with the situation?

By now, you, the reader, must feel somewhat overwhelmed, but do not fret. We will immediately deal with that by Summarizing the Concerns and Issues, actually the next column.

SUMMARIZE CONCERNS AND ISSUES (OR YOU'LL BE OVERWHELMED)

This may seem complex, since we elicited so many Concerns and Issues. So, it becomes necessary to Summarize them, or we become overloaded with too many details, unable to see the overall picture. Summarizing consolidates Concerns and Issues, helping point up overall patterns.

- Distrust hampers effective team functioning.
- Faculty lacks knowing and applying skills to team properly:
  - team building necessary
  - schisms:
    - Faculty members are apparently not accepting differences among each other—presently.
  - Some teams malfunctioning:
    - People do not know how to resolve conflict.
    - We have to reduce the "them/us" mentality.
    - Size of teams is a contributing factor.
- Size of school is contributing to concerns, distrust, alienation.
- Communication with administration, across and among teams and grade levels is insufficient, short-circuiting cooperation and coordination.
- Community experiencing socioeconomic changes:
  - more immigrants
  - greater cultural diversity arising, creating communications, understanding, acceptance issues
  - community participation declining
- Heightened feelings are creating problems with interpreting, *accepting others, generating distrust.*
- People have strong needs for recognition, acceptance, autonomy.
- There is conflict over which curriculum to use.

DIG OUT UNDERLYING THEMES (SEE COLUMN 3)

Analyzing for *Underlying Themes* makes potential for action easier, since fewer Themes exist than Summary items and that helps point up the "big picture."

- Trust/mistrust. Trust is essential for an organization to thrive.
- Unification and consistency is necessary, interpersonal strife is causing tension/mistrust.
- Teams are developing problems and need support to improve, such as team-building, conflict-resolution exercises:
  ○ excessive bickering, struggles for control
- The size of teams and school are generating problems. We need to decentralize to teams, create SLCs (Sullivan and Glanz 2006).
- The changing community is changing student attitudes toward school; parent participation is declining.
- Multicultural planning is needed.
- We humans need recognition.
- Curriculum needs to develop in a unified direction.

Themes also help discern underlying dimensions to achieve action, essential for focusing efforts.

DEVELOP POTENTIAL LINES OF ACTION/INITIATIVES

Now that we've analyzed Concerns and Issues, Summarized them, and uncovered Underlying Themes, we have a flow of analysis. This next flow, developing Potential Lines of Action/Initiatives (potential remedies) in this Analysis of Dynamics of Organizational Change strategy, is based on the preceding analysis of Underlying Themes.

The following comprise Potential Lines of Action or Initiatives:

- Develop trust-building exercises
- Develop team-building and conflict-resolution exercises
- Implement exercises to help people understand and accept each other, such as the Gregorc Style Delineator (1982)
- Open lines of communications; make communication a riveting priority (Barnard 1938)
- Develop Lines of Action to decentralize to teams and SLCs:
  ○ produces more people included in ownership, recognition, teaming, communication

- ○ reduces team size (from eight to four)
- ○ decentralization personalizes, since we deal with fewer people, units are smaller, so we get to know each other better
- ○ reduces conflict
- Develop major parent-involvement effort:
  - ○ establish a Multicultural Planning Committee
- Develop a major Recognition Program for everyone
- Establish a curriculum-steering committee

UNDERLYING RATIONALE FOR EACH
POTENTIAL LINE OF ACTION

Reflective Question

Why develop a rationale?

Dewey (1938) and a host of others note that theory usually underlies successful action, and that theory is highly practical. It is necessary to develop a Rationale to support each Potential Line of Action.

- Develop Trust
  - ○ The underlying rationale for developing trust is: cooperation rests on trust. If you distrust someone or an organization, you cannot work effectively with that person or organization you feel you must watch carefully (Bryk and Schneider 2002).
- Team Building
  - ○ Team building is essential for teams to function more effectively and efficiently, as are conflict-resolution techniques. Burying anger and other emotions, which elementary faculties frequently do, impedes constructing healthy relationships and organizational processes. People at first felt this was painful.
- Using a Personality Style Instrument for team building, improving understanding, acceptance, and communication
  - ○ Implementing a personality-style instrument exercise has never failed to help most people become more aware, accepting, and respecting of themselves, others, parents, students, siblings, administrators, authority figures—virtually everyone. Administering the Gregorc Style Delineator (1982) facilitated faculty to understand and to accept each other. People realized that the other person was not doing something to spite or to challenge them, but that that was their way of reacting as a personality to situations.

CONSEQUENCES/OUTCOMES

It is clear that the *Organizational Mapping* process did perform its purpose.

- It uncovered dynamics the organization was generating so that we could diagnose, analyze, and implement changes to achieve goals.
- Implementing the Gregorc was effective in facilitating considerably improved faculty understanding and acceptance of themselves and of each other. Additionally, styles of each staff member were listed.
- Trust-building exercises helped improve trust—open discussion reduced distrust.
- Team-building exercises fulfilled their goal.
- Relationships among teachers from the other school and those from Southwood Elementary had improved so much by the beginning of the Fall semester that distrust had completely disappeared.
- The teacher from that group, who served on the planning committee, said, "All we wanted was to be happy," which struck a chord; that ended the issue.
- Focusing intently on making sure that we communicated discoveries of the Planning Committee to everyone paid off handsomely, since no one possibly could feel left out. Shortly after the end of each meeting, everyone had duplicated minutes in hand. Direct, short lines of communication were established (as Barnard [1938] indicated).
- Decentralization into SLCs and teams moved ahead.
- Team sizes were reduced from eight to four.
- The Planning Committee unanimously agreed people were free to choose to team—or not.
- A major parent-involvement program developed, including a Multicultural Planning Committee and a Community Partnership Committee.
- A major recognition program was developed, implemented by a huge "Southwood Bulletin Board" placed in an area with heavy traffic, run by a Recognition Committee.
- A better sense of community among staff was promoted with a "Wonderful Wednesday" monthly program, each sponsored by a different team, who devised clever names for themselves, designing different activities for each session.
- A curriculum structure was devised to generate curriculum *as a routine*.

ANALYSIS

More Results

Analyzing the Gregorc provided an outlet for humor as people became more familiar with idiosyncrasies individual personalities generate. People were able to laugh at themselves. For example, asking strongly concrete sequential people how they shop at a grocery store might elicit the response that their shopping lists are organized by the store's aisles, to which the abstract random people respond with gales of laughter (they lose their lists—if ever bothering to make them). They are perfectionists, loners.

Reflective Question

Whenever a party is to be organized, whom do you expect will volunteer?

Of course the abstract random people will love to do it, will have lots of food, loud music, hordes of people. They love to work with others. The concrete sequential people? They will not want to come but will come on time, hide in a corner hating the loud music, and leave first.

Reflective Question

Who will love to fix any piece of equipment?

The concrete random person, who will take it apart to see how it works, but will often bandwagon to another of his many projects, not bother putting it back together again. (It's too boring.)

The abstract sequential person is a reader, thinks deeply, is a great analyst—a loner. We overheard teachers teasing the principal (a very strong abstract sequential personality) with, "I can tell it's your abstract sequential personality kicking in again. I know, you need to think about it, and then we can talk about it tomorrow." Her district superintendent approached every conference with, "Please don't talk to me about what you've been thinking. It just makes my brain hurt."

- Using Barnard's (1938) (the father of administration) three indispensable elements to all organizations—to improve the school (any organization) noted there are *three interacting elements indispensable* to an organization:
  - It must have a *common mission or purpose* (otherwise it goes nowhere).
  - It must have a *system of cooperation* to facilitate achieving the common mission.
  - It must have a *system of communication* to facilitate achieving the common purpose.

- The Gregorc helped establish a *system of cooperation,* increasing trust, eliminating suspicion.
- *Lines of communication* facilitated achieving a *common purpose.* Sending minutes with graphics illustrating these processes after each meeting to *everyone* was helpful. Providing everyone with the same information at the same time with full details allows for clarifying issues by those who did not attend. Without a common frame of reference, attempts to recall specifics of a meeting are usually misquoted, reinterpreted, or misunderstood.
- Barnard's three indispensable elements of an organization were met.
- The underlying Rationale for developing a *major parent-involvement program* is that it promotes *buy-in* by all involved.
- Using Maslow's Hierarchy of Needs:
  - Maslow's (1954) Hierarchy of Needs stresses the third needs level is *social*
  - people *need recognition and acceptance* (without it they become unfulfilled, and will begin going after it, sometimes in unacceptable ways).
- Developing a curriculum structure:
  - Developing a *curriculum structure* (chapter 4) enables a faculty *to generate curriculum as a routine,* avoiding needing a supreme effort to make one change. If people feel that curriculum can be changed *as a routine,* change can become normal, part of everyday functioning. You've essentially destroyed barriers resisting instituting any change—a rather remarkable outcome.

SUMMARY

The Analysis of Dynamics of Change process performed its functions admirably. Its Organizational Mapping diagnostic function uncovered key Concerns and Issues, which were Summarized. It analyzed Underlying Themes and pointed up Potential Lines of Action or Initiatives. It facilitated analyzing Rationales to evaluate potential lines of action, and was useful in evaluating the developed action Outcomes in terms of these rationales.

Chapter 12 provides insights into the impact of the constructivist strategy and elements of constructivism on the school three and five years later.

Reflective Questions

1. What is your first impression?
2. Do you admire the principal's courage? Note how she involved everyone.

3. How do you analyze the change model?
   A. What additional elements would you add?
   B. People were willing to confront issues head on, rather than dodg-
      ing them, as often occurs in many organizations (witness Enron's
      debacle). Why?
      a) What role did the principal play?
   C. What patterns did this organizational mapping change model un-
      cover? What patterns did it miss? How could it be improved?
   D. Do you like looking for themes underlying issues and concerns?
      What is the advantage?
4. What do you think of moving an entire school toward constructivism?
   Advantages? Disadvantages?
   A. Why did no opposition arise?

IMPORTANT TERMS

Analysis of Dynamics of Organizational Change—A bottom-up organizational change strategy focusing on dynamics/processes that gum
things up

Constructivism—A view of learning that recognizes that individuals actively construct their own meanings and understandings; knowledge is
made by the individual, not acquired

Lewinian change strategy—Unfreezing an organization's practice or structure, moving to a new level, and refreezing the change

Potential Lines of Action/Initiatives—Possible remedial courses of action
to deal with issues and concerns

Rationale—The underlying reason for choosing a course of action

Recognition program—A program designed to provide recognition for
achievement

12

Example 2, Continued: Success! Three (and, *Postscript, Now Five*) Years of Constructivism

Spectacular Changes—and the Scores Jumped Up (Still Perking, but Needing to Replan)

Courage leads toward the stars, fear toward death.

—Lucius Seneca, The Younger, *Hercules Furens*

Wisdom, compassion, and courage—these are the three universally recognized moral qualities of men.

—Confucius

There's nothing like a nice, longitudinal study to document change in an organization (particularly if it supports what you've done).

This does.

We started the constructivist change strategy three years earlier, reported in chapter 11. Dr. Isaacson then repeated the process three years later, using the Analysis of Dynamics of Change strategy (Burley and Shapiro 1994; Shapiro 1994; Shapiro, Benjamin, and Hunt 1995; Shapiro 2000) as reported in her dissertation (2004).

Joseph Brown (2006) studied the school two years later to determine whether the organizational entropy predicted by the Tri-Partite Theory of Organizational Change and Control (see chapter 6) was finessed with the internal organizational structures developed for Southwood.

The preceding chapter laid out Concerns and Issues brought to the table by the Planning Committee. The process included Summarizing those issues and concerns, teasing out Underlying Themes, then developing Potential

Lines of Action/Initiatives to deal with issues and concerns. The next step was to unearth Rationales for each alternative Line of Action (together with its theoretical base), and last, evaluate resulting Consequences.

Figure 11.1 from chapter 11 is the source for the following. Note the *issues*, unfortunately all too normal for any organization. These included issues of:

- distrust
- destructive rumors
- misunderstandings, schisms (them/us)
- fighting over curriculum based on faculty schisms
- communications problems
- struggles for control
- teams too large to manage, causing dissension
- people's feelings bruised
- changing community
- more immigrants with different languages and diverse cultures
- inadequate provision for recognition, among others

Now, let's take a look at figure 12.1, summarizing Concerns and Issues expressed *three years later*. Note that old issues and concerns fade, are far fewer—and for the better.

Differences are considerable and deep—some would say spectacular. We are looking at quite a different school:

- Collaboration, never mentioned, is perceived as continuing and essential, often during lunch.
- They want to continue the positive climate and culture.
- They want to continue trust-building—built by spending time together.
- They want to continue efforts to communicate.
- They want to continue relationships-building; teachers respect each other—they offer support.
- They want to ensure that new teachers have a strong support system—never mentioned before. They believe it is important for new teachers to develop a constructivist philosophy.
- They want continuous articulation of curriculum.

Each column is fundamentally changed—for the better.

Look at the differences in column 3, *Underlying Themes*, best summarized by Lynne Menard, quoted at the beginning of chapter 11:

"Help me, I'm drowning."

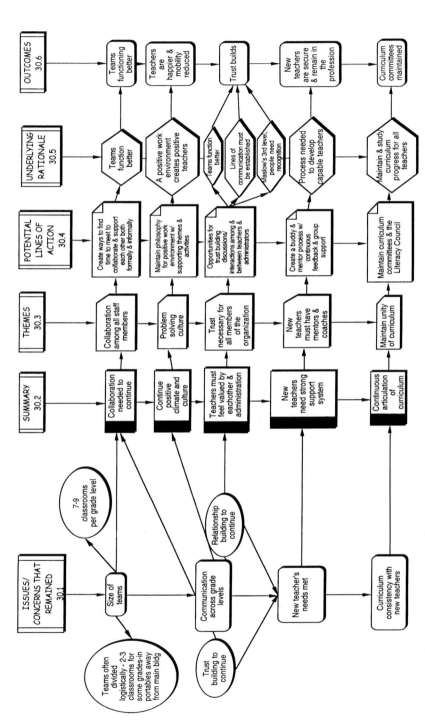

Figure 12.1. Analysis of Dynamics of Organizational Change: Three Years Later

The earlier column is rife with concern about trust/mistrust, interpersonal strife, dysfunctional teams, jealousy, hostility, changing student attitudes toward education, and needs for recognition, and parent participation.

Positive Themes

Column three, *Underlying Themes*, in figure 12.1 talks of:

- Collaboration to continue
- A problem-solving culture being built
- Trust essential to success
- Concern that new teachers have mentors and coaches
- Maintaining unity of curriculum

Note what is *not* there—distrust, interpersonal friction and strife, alienation, dysfunctional teams, concern about changing student attitudes toward education, desire for greater parent participation (increased substantially), and needs for personal recognition.

New concerns focused on professional issues, not egocentric, self-focused needs—far fewer to generate dysfunctions.

Potential Lines of Action/Initiatives—Very Supportive

Differences in column 4, *Potential Lines of Action/Initiatives*, reveal fundamental differences. The earlier column wants initiatives to improve trust, cooperation, and team building using a personality-style instrument so people understand and accept each other, develop a process to recognize anyone doing anything significant, develop a Multicultural Planning Committee to deal proactively with incoming people from different cultures, and develop a curriculum committee to facilitate everyone working on a similar curriculum.

Let's look at Potential Lines of Action/Initiatives three years later:

- Create ways to find time to meet to collaborate and support each other formally and informally, often at each others' houses. Use FISH (the Seattle Fish Market approach to making work fun), the Gregorc Personality Style Delineator, and "Wonderful Wednesdays" for staff get-togethers
- Maintain philosophy for positive work environment with supporting themes and activities. "Newbies" need support, mentoring—and get it
- Develop opportunities for trust-building discussions among and between teachers and leaders

- Create a buddy/mentor process with continuous feedback and group support for new teachers, especially in integrating curriculum
- Maintain curriculum committees and the Literacy Council
- Establish a clear constructivist philosophy
- Teams sit in interviews to determine if prospective teachers chosen can fit in and practice constructivist philosophy approaches
- Teams organize themselves—and the school
- In addition, teachers want to individualize staff development
- The faculty wants to cultivate teachers as leaders

These dimensions include:
  - Collaboration
  - Trust-building, forming relationships
  - Asked for help, received it
  - Value of personality styles
  - Value of positive attitude
  - Took on leadership roles

The faculty moved into professional strategies to continue improving. The Literacy Council is new, as is maintaining the philosophy, never mentioned earlier. Collaboration was a dream, supporting each other was never mentioned earlier. Mentoring new teachers was not on the radar, nor was coaching them.

OUTCOMES THREE YEARS LATER

Let's take a look at the large number of Outcomes, the last column in figure 12.1.

- The organization's dynamics were uncovered, providing opportunity to deal with issues and concerns.
- The personality-style instrument improved trust and acceptance.
- Team-building exercises worked.
- Relationships among people from different schools improved.
- Communication patterns improved.

Decentralizing into SLCs

- Decentralizing into teams and SLCs worked
- Team sizes reduced
- Teaming optional, depending on teacher readiness
- A major parent involvement program initiated
- A Multicultural Planning Committee started
- A major recognition program initiated (shades of Maslow)

- Wonderful Wednesday monthly programs promoted sense of community
- A curriculum structure developed to generate curriculum *as a routine*

The teacher recognition program worked like a charm. Next, the Multicultural Planning Committee sponsored an evening event in which kids and parents (by then over fifty different nationalities and cultures) brought in a small tapestry identifying key items revealing their culture. The faculty expected at most a hundred, and were stunned as over 680 were brought in. These then served as the stage backdrop, covering it from wall to wall.

From a large number of Outcomes earlier, we find a handful three years later in figure 12.1.

- The constructivist strategy worked.
- Teams and SLCs are functioning better.
- Teachers expressed their happiness directly—teacher mobility evaporated.
- Trust kept building—they worked at it.
- New teachers are more secure, want to stay in teaching.
- Curriculum committees continue their work.
- Teachers are cultivated as leaders.
- A constructivist philosophy was established, driving the school.

Development of Key Supportive Internal Structures (SLCs and PLCs)

- SLCs developed.
- PLCs formed, supporting new and veteran faculty.
- Test results on state tests improved significantly.

These are relatively profound professional changes. The school obviously adopted a constructivist philosophy and articulated it. Their focus is on relationships among themselves, since they are a team and SLC operation, with a variety of team and nongraded models used. And their focus is on improving kids' education.

Themes and Indicators

Isaacson developed themes and indicators from the study. See table 12.1.

Building a Constructivist Philosophy

This comprises a key to reforming the school. Teachers clearly recognized that they had to understand the philosophy, that it was the driving force for

Table 12.1. Themes and Indicators Underlying Teachers' Perceptions

Code	Theme / Sub-Topic	Identifying Indicators
CP	**Constructivist Philosophy**	Use of the constructivist vision, higher order thinking, thinking "outside of the box", a non-prescriptive curriculum
CP1.	Sub-topics Understanding the concept	Thinking about thinking; **metacognitive skills**; probing to think on my own; figure things out; not given an answer, but justify my solution; find the problem; explain, constructing our own knowledge

(Isaacson indicated that overlapping indicators exist among constructivism, problem solving and decision-making concepts)

Code	Theme / Sub-Topic	Identifying Indicators
CP2.	Problem solving, decision making	Questions, find ways to make it better, Principal asked what I want to do, think first, plan, answers not given
CP3.	Reflective practice	Discuss what happened, explain why, do it better next time, examine, pre-requisite skills, dig deeper, look back, then look forward
CP4.	Risk-free environment	Try it out, experiment, if it doesn't work, try again, work it out, think creatively
CP5.	Learner-centered	How children learn, think of kids first, observe, listen, watch, provide opportunities, life-long learning, creative approach, kids can explain their thinking
C	**Change**	Movement, disruption, anticipation of something being different from before
C1.	Evolution of curriculum	Understanding—math, integrated units, any subject area changes as learned, finding better ways to instruct, resistance/excitement, adding on/substituting new strategies
C2.	Change of models	**Vertical team** concept (multi-grading), resistance/excitement, **looping** concept
C3.	Change of teams	Disruption when someone leaves/joins teams, teachers choosing to move seen as negative/positive experience
L	**Leadership**	Focus on the principal, negative/positive experience
L1.	Support of teachers	Feel supported, provided with ideas, suggestions, help with students and with parents, not threatened by interaction, empowers us, trusts us to make decisions

(*continued*)

Table 12.1.   (*Continued*)

Code	Theme / Sub-Topic	Identifying Indicators
L2.	Feeling appreciated	Spends time making teachers feel appreciated, recognized publicly and in private, complimentary
L3.	Provides a professional work environment	Provided materials and supplies because teachers need them, values input into what teachers want, provided time to work with teammates, feel comfortable, feel safe
TL	***Teachers as Leaders***	Isaacson assumed that all items identified relating to team building belonged in this category. If someone initiates a group getting together or organizes a group project, a leader is recognized
TL1.	Collaboration	Collaboration, getting together as a group, planning together, working together
TL2.	Trust-building, forming relationships	I like my team, like working with my pod members, work well together, get along, know value of communication, became a team
TL3.	Asked for help, received it	Willing to ask for help, teachers help me
TL4.	Value of personality styles	Understand each other, understand myself, easier to work with people, laugh at formerly perceived irritants
TL5.	Value of positive attitude	FISH (Seattle Fish Market Model of having fun) helped me, attitude of play, make their day, importance of positive attitude
TL6.	Took on leadership roles	Leadership, mentor, committee work/ chair
A	***Affect***	Feeling words: happy, love, excited, family

practice. They also perceived that problem solving, decision making, and reflection underlay putting the constructivist philosophy into operation. And the environment had to be risk-free; teachers had to feel safe (again, shades of Maslow's second level) to be able to be learner-centered.

Change

The second theme for Isaacson is change. Note that people felt that when teachers left the team it was disruptive. Yet changing the structure of the school and the curriculum, while disruptive, was perceived as positive.

Leadership

For a book such as this on leadership, this theme certainly is central. The theme has three indicators, the third of which is not too evident in some leadership literature. The first two, supporting teachers and feeling appreciated, deal with interpersonal feelings, which are often ignored by "cold-prickly" administrators. But they are central to a supportive environment, as is the last, providing a professional work environment.

This latter focuses on providing materials and supplies because teachers need them, provide time for teams to work, without which they cannot function. The indicators point to a sensitivity to the underlying conditions necessary to facilitate teams and individuals to work effectively.

Teachers as Leaders

This theme also bursts with the interpersonal, as well as the organizational. Note that teachers liked their teams, the central role of trust, and being open to each other to ask for help, which increases the effectiveness of collaboration. This constitutes a "leadership density" factor, which increases the leadership base of the organization and builds leadership experience over a wider net of people.

Teacher's Affect

This theme was totally unanticipated, but told us that the teachers loved being in the school, and even felt that they had constructed their family. Indeed, when some supplies needed to be wrapped up and sent back to a supplier immediately, the secretary called, "Will the family please come to the office and help pack? We have a very tight deadline." All the teachers dropped what they were doing and went immediately.

Conclusions and Implications

Isaacson then drew several conclusions and implications:

1. Constructivism can be used as an educational organizational change model to reform an entire elementary school and implement a constructivist philosophy and practices.
2. Teachers believe that standardized test scores can increase from teaching constructivistically—test scores supported this. See Appendix A.
3. To make the school resistant to organizational entropy, a maintenance plan is necessary, with replanning every two to three years to continue the process. The SLCs and PLCs are essential to this.

4. It is crucial to recognize the importance of teachers' perceptions in creating an organizational culture with constructivist educational practices.
5. The role of the principal is pivotal. The principal must believe in and model constructivism (Isaacson 2004, v).

POSTSCRIPT: A FOLLOW-UP STUDY
TWO YEARS LATER—SUCCESS!

Two years later, Joseph Brown (2006) conducted a follow-up study to determine whether the school was able to continue its constructivist philosophy and educational practices. Brown based his study first on Isaacson's recommendation that the school be studied after two or three years to determine if the constructivist philosophy and educational practices were able to continue.

The second reason for his study was to determine whether the school could build internal structures or mechanisms or replan to retain the constructivist philosophy and practices. The Tri-Partite Theory (chapter 6) maintains that unless such internal replanning structures or actual replanning occurs every two or three years, the program will be lost. That is, the iron forces of entropy will inevitably destroy any plan in a relatively short time unless the organization replans or develops internal structures to maintain the plan.

Brown found that the leadership and faculty of Southwood did, indeed, do exactly that. The faculty decentralized into SLCs and developed PLCs (Clauset 2008). In addition, faculty chose as Isaacson's replacement her former assistant principal over candidates, some of whom had no idea what constructivism looked like. Together, they created a mentoring program for new teachers and others, with half-day pullouts for new teachers as a mentoring device.

The SLCs and PLCs with the mentoring features essentially function as self-renewing strategies to undo the hovering forces of entropy.

Summary

Constructivism can be used as an educational organizational change model to reform an entire school and implement a constructivist philosophy and practices. Normal dysfunctional issues and concerns (jealousy, conflict, distrust, competition, etc.) that dominated the faculty literally disappeared, replaced by concern for supporting each other, and for mentoring new teachers to improve their teaching and feelings of support and success. Teachers bought into constructivism strongly and forced the hiring of a principal who supported the philosophy, their levels of satisfaction clearly manifested. Test scores improved significantly.

As a consequence, the school developed a wide reputation in a very large county district as singular, unique—and very good.

IMPORTANT TERMS

FISH—a game developed by the Seattle Fish Market to make work more fun, adapted by Southwood

Constructivism—a view of learning that recognizes that individuals actively construct their own meanings and understandings. Knowledge is made by the individual, not acquired

13

Example 3: Making a Large Inner-City High School Work by Decentralizing It—Steering It Through the Currents

A school should be small enough so that students aren't redundant.

—Roger G. Barker and Paul V. Gump, *Big School, Small School*

THE PROCESS LAID OUT

The culture of large, inner-city high schools resists change—anyone who knows anything about high schools usually agrees wholeheartedly with that statement. (Actually, virtually any high school's culture resists change pretty successfully.) Sarason (1996) in his revision of his classic book on organizational change, even titled his work, *Revisiting "The Culture of the School and the Problem of Change,"* attesting to the difficulty of pulling off such a transformation. Not only that, but his key chapter modified his title significantly into "The Culture of the School and the Problem of *Social* Change."

Reflective Question

What do we mean by saying that any change is social?

Sarason was telling us that it is not enough to talk about change in organizations, but that *any change is social in nature* in any organization, not just schools, and, therefore, has to deal with all sorts of social issues caroming around the room when people get together (Hensley 1982), such as:

- Who has power and control—and who doesn't
- Who is accepted and who is rejected (and, will *I* be rejected?)
- Conflict over goals (and, are the goals worthwhile?)
- Jealousy
- Prestige
- Hidden agendas

These are just a few of the dynamics in groups and why pulling off any social change is hard.

USING THE ANALYSIS OF THE DYNAMICS OF INDIVIDUALIZED ORGANIZATIONAL CHANGE: A DIAGNOSTIC, ANALYTICAL, PLANNING, AND IMPLEMENTATION STRATEGY

So, what did we do?

This social change approach utilized a *constructivist change strategy*, that is, a bottom-up approach to make fundamental changes in an inner city high school in Pinellas County, Florida. (See chapter 9 for a brief description, and the three preceding chapters before this one [10, 11, and 12] for a detailed account of using the Analysis of the Dynamics of Individualized Organizational Change [Burley & Shapiro 1994; Shapiro 1994; Shapiro 2000; Shapiro, Benjamin & Hunt 1995] in pulling off that strategy in a middle and an elementary school.) We used the same change strategy in this high school, again quite successfully.

In the Beginning: The Principal

This Lewinian-based (1952) (see chapter 9) change strategy started when the principal, new to the school and an energetic change agent, asked me as an outside consultant to try to help the faculty meet the educational and emotional needs of students and staff. He and I had met in a couple of classes I taught, and his wife subsequently (and foolishly) had taken a couple of classes, also. He had asked me to serve on his son's master's thesis committee. So we knew each other and had a good deal of mutual respect.

When he asked me to meet with him, I wondered why he hadn't been promoted to an assistant superintendency—he was that good. He was both well organized and a "big picture" thinker as well.

Of course, first I asked about issues and concerns he perceived operating, then laid out the strategy portrayed in chapter 9 and the following chapters, using the Analysis of Dynamics of Individualized Organizational Change strategy. After agreeing that it seemed to be quite useful, we agreed to ask the major indigenous leader of the school to come in and confer about this potential change initiative, together with the new assistant principal, whose role seemed to be operations officer.

Bringing in the Indigenous Leader: His Insights

Reflective Question

Why did we do that?

After discussing this objective with the indigenous leader, who was a high-profile music teacher generating several major productions yearly, and his sidekick associate, as well as the new assistant principal, we asked for their diagnosis of major issues and concerns they saw for the school. They had started dividing the school into SLCs, which included two preexisting, older magnets plus three new SLCs with different themes.

They were having a dickens of a time keeping teachers only teaching in one SLC, which they called making the schedule pure. (I wondered if this was possible—or desirable, but had to get more data.) Neither students nor teachers had developed a sense of identity that they belonged to any SLC, although they had done so in the two magnets.

Another issue raised among others, was that this had been the District/County's first African American high school, still was a slight majority black student-wise school, low socioeconomic status (SES) for that population, with a plurality of black faculty, and was doing poorly on the state's version of the annual NCLB test, called the Florida Comprehensive Assessment Test (FCAT). The two magnets had been designed to attract upper-middle-class white students, which had been quite successful.

Another considerable concern expressed was that the school was being forced to move into a brand new high school during the winter holiday season, much to the dismay of the faculty and principal, who wanted to wait until the summer. Preparation for this was screwing them up royally. (The Central Office and Board, after that ordeal was over, concluded that they would avoid such a decision in the future.)

Last, the music teacher indicated that the faculty wanted fast action; they didn't want to palaver endlessly. My response to the impatience was that unless we found out what issues and concerns the faculty felt were important, we could not be effective in dealing with them, and that I had a strategy to do just that. So, I briefly laid out the change strategy.

First, a Planning Committee

The music teacher was mildly trustful of this, particularly since he clearly had a great deal of respect for the principal, who said that he knew I had worked in environments like this. The principal and I indicated that to pull anything off, we needed a sizeable planning task force which had to represent all relevant social systems.

Key Elements

I laid out key elements in the planning process.
But, first, two Reflective Questions:

1. Why not focus on problems people faced, instead of Concerns and Issues?
2. Why make sure every major group (social system) was involved?
   - Concerns and Issues people felt
   - Summarize them so we could work with them
   - Look for Underlying Themes
   - Develop some Potential Lines of Action
   - Analyze Rationales for each Line of Action
   - *Implement* and *analyze* Consequences

The music teacher thought this might work, so we put our heads together and he suggested a number of potential representatives from key faculty and student reference groups (at least one from each SLC, and not all goody two-shoes from the Student Council). Faculty included administrators, the new assistant principal, another assistant principal, and representatives from each department, SLC, magnet, and someone from the office.

Since the music instructor had been at the school for years and had excellent relations with large parts of the community, he was able to suggest several key community and central office representatives as well. We tried to get people from the central office who had clout and who would be supportive, plus the woman who headed up a grant for five high schools, all with large disadvantaged populations, to facilitate them moving into SLCs.

Since I had chaired a number of doctoral committees, taught graduate courses in the county, and had done in-service sessions in the county, I could contribute with a degree of expertise. They suggested involving the rest of the assistant principals next.

We then met the assistant principals in talking about objectives. There were some interesting issues and concerns raised, although I could tell that a couple of assistant principals were not sure about me, or even about the principal. They also came up with a list of names; we then contacted the people on the list for our first meeting to be held early in December before the winter holiday break, when the Great Move was scheduled to take place.

Starting

The Planning Committee/Task Force met for the entire morning, starting with a breakfast, broke for refreshments briefly, and worked until about 11:30, at which time they had lunch and went back to classes. At first we had introductions, after which I explained that we would ask about Concerns and Issues people had, and that we would take plenty of time to hear everyone. I'd try to Summarize and then look for Underlying Themes. I began to lay out people's responses on large sheets of 24" × 36" newsprint on the wall.

We generated about fifty to sixty items, which caused me to keep on taping sheets together with masking tape so that we had a document about nine feet long hanging on the wall. People hung around and talked, including the music teacher/leader. A lot of interesting dynamics surfaced during the interactions, but people focused on the issues. There was a good deal of reflecting as the Concerns and Issues unfolded.

My job was to elicit the Concerns and Issues, then after the meeting to Summarize them, and next analyze the Underlying Themes. I did this also on the large newsprint so that the analysis picked up issues, then laid out a related underlying theme with an arrow from the issue. The analysis certainly looked logical (at least to me).

The Impact of the "Great Move" into the New Building over the Winter Holidays

However, suspecting changes in attitudes to develop from the move into the new large building from the really decrepit old facility, I came back right after the holiday break before the next scheduled meeting of the Planning Committee/Task Force and wandered about the halls. I had coffee with faculty members, administrators, coordinators, clerks, and custodians; talked with the few students I met in halls, but more in the cafeteria; and then went back and talked with the principal and the music teacher.

When I showed up at the door of his class and watched the kids rehearse, I was quite impressed with their professionalism and self-direction—and said so. He was able to pull out of his class, since they were rehearsing for a show and were virtually autonomous in their practicing. He still indicated that faculty were impatient, didn't want to fool around, and wanted action.

My response was that this was a totally different school—that kids weren't hanging out in halls, weren't trying to hide in nooks and crannies, that the school had essentially changed—drastically—and for the better. People were smiling, kids were upbeat, teachers looked happier, administrators didn't look harried, harassed, and hurried.

THE ANALYSIS

He thought about it and agreed, as did his colleague, and so did the principal. I brought in the newsprint sheets with the first run-through of Concerns and Issues, with the arrows on newsprint laid side-by-side leading to the Underlying Themes. And next to the themes, on another long set of newsprint, I drew arrows to some Potential Lines of Action.

They liked the analysis, and agreed to repeat the process of teasing out issues and concerns, but said to be aware that faculty patience was short; although they were extremely happy with the new (and fairly luxurious) facility, they did not want to waste any time. (Clearly, the music teacher still was not too sure of me, but as a positive sign, was trying to be helpful.)

I then presented the Underlying Themes and Potential Lines of Action on the large newsprint, to the great interest of the folks present. I repeated my comment that this a new and different school and then repeated asking about Concerns and Issues, ending with easily eighty items, many different from the first go-through. Next, I was to look for new Underlying Themes, suggest adding some Potential Lines of Action to deal with the Concerns and Issues and Underlying Themes, which we could modify and add to at the next meeting. We set a new time to meet two weeks ahead.

It *was* a totally different school.

The Concerns and Issues were quite substantial, but different from the first time—and, I thought, honest and realistic. As I pored over the huge welter of Concerns and Issues, the following Underlying Themes or categories seemed to emerge, so I focused on them, jumping over my usual second step of summarizing right into teasing out the Underlying Themes, since I wanted people to feel that we were making a great deal of progress, and wanted to finesse the impatience.

Underlying Themes

Reflective Question

Why bother with themes?

Underlying Themes fell into the following categories:

- *Kids* are changing, which is impacting the school culture
- Which has an impact on *Student-Teacher Relationships*
- This requires changing *Teaching Practices*

- Which has major *Implications for Curriculum*
- *Parent/Community Relationships* need addressing pronto
- To work more effectively, *Administrative Teams for each SLC* that work are required
- A *Miscellaneous (grab bag)* category emerged

This analysis, presented on the large chart paper sheets, connected with lines from the original eighty plus Concerns and Issues provided the grist of the day's discussions. I had also laid out related Potential Lines of Action with a handful of underlying Rationales and then Solutions/Lines of Action and Next Steps. This was on double sheets of 17" × 11" paper so that everyone had these relatively crude tables to look at—and to keep.

People thought and reflected for a goodly chunk of time. One outcome: impatience disappeared. People really got involved in heavy-duty discussion. We had overcome.

The Next Step: Figuring Out Potential Lines of Action

Eight Potential Lines of Action had emerged, each developing from an Underlying Theme. The group agreed to adopt these as our plan of action:

- Rebuild the *school culture*
- Implement the *ninth-grade SLC*
- *Develop/build SLC teams*; develop *PLCs*
- *Implement curriculum* involving kids, community, possibly using a curriculum structure
- *Community/school relationships* need focus; multicultural focus
- Need *Recognition Committee* to recognize everyone (shades of Maslow)
- *SLC leadership teams* (one for each SLC) need developing
- *Implement grant* (to get funding for equipment and the Summer Institute)

Underlying Rationales

Reflective Question

Why bother? Does theory guide practice? (It does in medicine; what about education?)

The underlying Rationales for each Potential Line of Action were also added. Rationales were essentially the theoretical underpinning for each Line of Action. (After all, we are college professors, and this substantiates each action selected.) For example, building the school culture is essential to reform the school, based on numerous authorities, such as Linton

(1955) in his *Tree of Culture*. This cannot be left to chance, or dysfunctional results might occur (Oxley 1989).

Note that the organizing principle for the work was that each Underlying Theme (e.g., Kids Changing, Student–Teacher Relationships), served as the vehicle for laying out each category of issues and concerns, followed by underlying themes, etc.

When I met with the music teacher, his sidekick, the principal, and the assistant principal to set up the next meeting, they were pleased with the results, and felt that the Planning Committee would feel the same way. Next, we believed that people would want a *timeline* to construct an overall plan, as well as a summer in-service education program.

Next Steps: Planning—and Results

The minutes with my crude tables went out to everyone, so that the next meeting in February began to deal with Next Steps. At the final "Summing Up: What Have We Accomplished?" portion of the meeting, people agreed, "We are moving forward—and developing our plan." People wanted to focus on the resources available in the central office and pull them in to help. They wanted to continue a focus on developing student leadership—and did, by supporting an existent program.

And the Planning Committee agreed that the eight Lines of Action were our plan to implement. We had the plan.

The music teacher was given carte blanche to work with the central office grant coordinator to implement the grant and get orders for equipment and materials in. The grant was also to be used to support the summer in-service program, which the music teacher agreed to coordinate. A Subplanning Council was formally established consisting of the principal, assistant principal, music teacher and his associate, and me.

In the meantime, I had contacted a near-genius graphic artist, Diana Trees, who had diagrammed the results of the Analysis of Dynamics of Organizational Change for Southwood Elementary School (see chapters 11 and 12) using the *Inspiration* software program. She produced figures 13.1 through 13.7, which were handed out to everyone before the next meeting.

This led to a flurry of activity of implementing plans and developing subplans. Table 13.1, "Action Plan," demonstrates the eight Lines of Action that were developed.

For example, a group went full steam ahead in planning the ninth-grade SLC. Another group focused on building SLC teams of those teachers who wanted to work in teams. The music teacher pulled a small group together to develop the Summer Institute. The newish Deputy Superintendent had heard about the action going on (actually, I called her) and came before the next meeting to see the newsprint sheets hung on the walls and examined them very carefully. Impressed, she gave her imprimatur to the operation, an approval everyone took to heart.

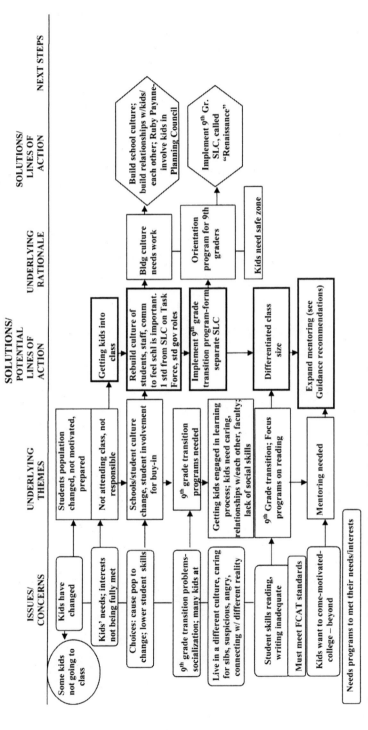

Figure 13.1. Analysis of dynamics of organizational changes—students

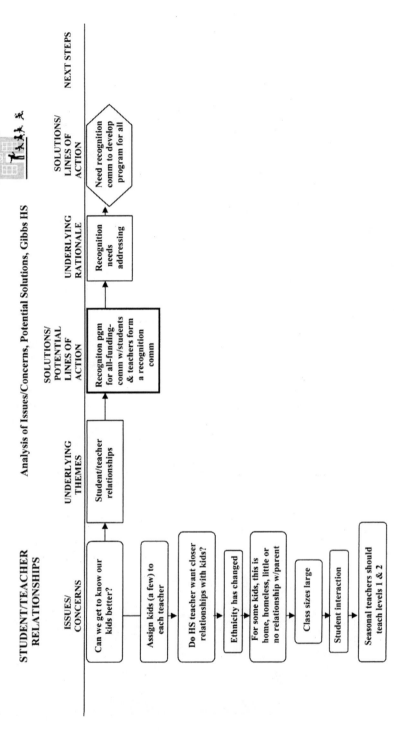

STUDENT/TEACHER RELATIONSHIPS

Analysis of Issues/Concerns, Potential Solutions, Gibbs HS

ISSUES/ CONCERNS	UNDERLYING THEMES	SOLUTIONS/ POTENTIAL LINES OF ACTION	UNDERLYING RATIONALE	SOLUTIONS/ LINES OF ACTION	NEXT STEPS

- Can we get to know our kids better?
- Assign kids (a few) to each teacher
- Do HS teacher want closer relationships with kids?
- Ethnicity has changed
- For some kids, this is home, homeless, little or no relationship w/parent
- Class sizes large
- Student interaction
- Seasonal teachers should teach levels 1 & 2

Student/teacher relationships

Recogniton pgm for all-funding-comm w/students & teachers form a recognition comm

Recognition needs addressing

Need recognition comm to develop program for all

Figure 13.2. Analysis of dynamics of organizational change—student/teacher relationships

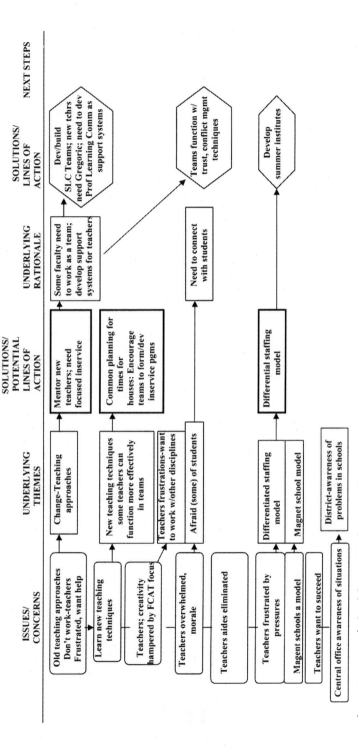

Figure 13.3. Analysis of dynamics of organizational change—teaching approaches

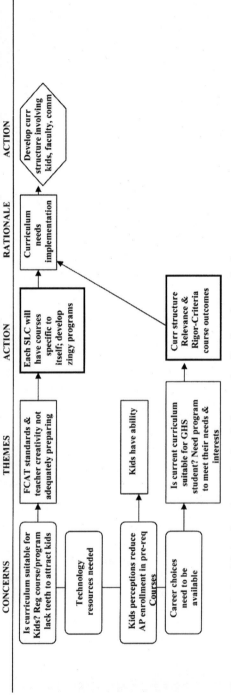

Analysis of Issues/Concerns, Potential Solutions, Gibbs HS

IMPLICATIONS FOR CURRICULUM

| ISSUES/ CONCERNS | UNDERLYING THEMES | SOLUTIONS/ POTENTIAL LINES OF ACTION | UNDERLYING RATIONALE | SOLUTIONS/ LINES OF ACTION | NEXT STEPS |

Is curriculum suitable for Kids? Reg course/program lack teeth to attract kids

FCAT standards & teacher creativity not adequately preparing

Each SLC will have courses specific to itself; develop zingy programs

Curriculum needs implementation

Develop curr structure involving kids, faculty, comm

Technology resources needed

Kids perceptions reduce AP enrollment in pre-req Courses

Kids have ability

Career choices need to be available

Is current curriculum suitable for GHS student? Need program to meet their needs & interests

Curr structure Relevance & Rigor-Criteria course outcomes

Figure 13.4. Analysis of dynamics of organizational change—implications for curriculum

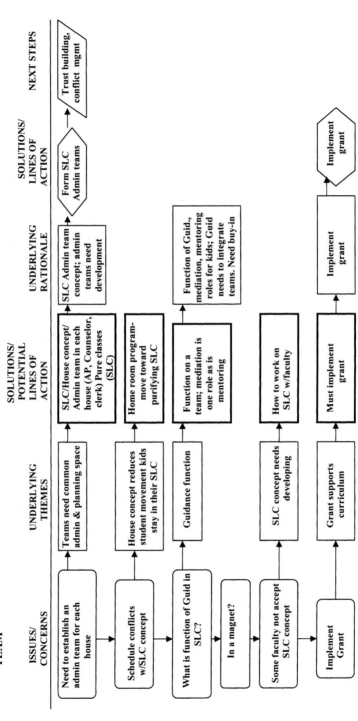

Figure 13.5. Analysis of dynamics of organizational change—administrative team

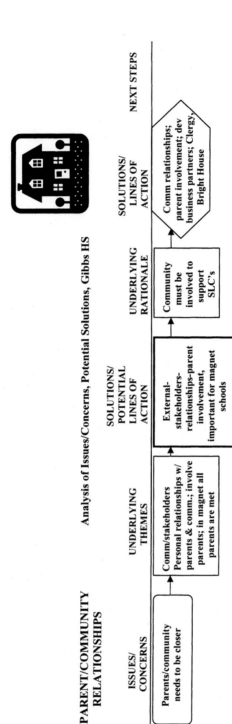

PARENT/COMMUNITY RELATIONSHIPS

Analysis of Issues/Concerns, Potential Solutions, Gibbs HS

ISSUES/ CONCERNS	UNDERLYING THEMES	SOLUTIONS/ POTENTIAL LINES OF ACTION	UNDERLYING RATIONALE	SOLUTIONS/ LINES OF ACTION	NEXT STEPS
Parents/community needs to be closer	Comm/stakeholders Personal relationships w/ parents & comm.; involve parents; in magnet all parents are met	External-stakeholders-relationships-parent involvement, important for magnet schools	Community must be involved to support SLC's	Comm relationships; parent involvement; dev business partners; Clergy, Bright House	

Figure 13.6. Analysis of dynamics organizational change—parent/community relationships

MISCELLANEOUS

Analysis of Issues/Concerns, Potential Solutions, Gibbs HS

ISSUES/ CONCERNS	UNDERLYING THEMES	SOLUTIONS/ POTENTIAL LINES OF ACTION	UNDERLYING RATIONALE	SOLUTIONS/ LINES OF ACTION	NEXT STEPS

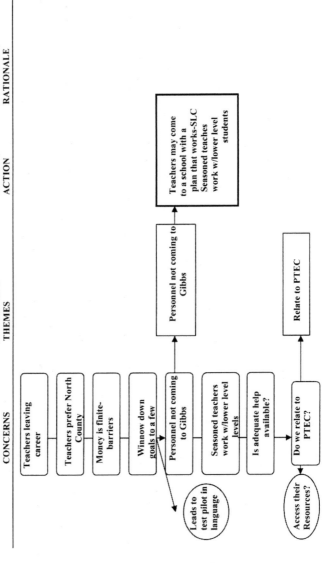

Teachers leaving career

Teachers prefer North County

Money is finite–barriers

Winnow down goals to a few

Personnel not coming to Gibbs

Seasoned teachers work w/lower level levels

Is adequate help available?

Do we relate to PTEC?

Leads to test pilot in language

Access their Resources?

Personnel not coming to Gibbs

Teachers may come to a school with a plan that works–SLC Seasoned teaches work w/lower level students

Relate to PTEC

Figure 13.1.   Analysis of dynamics of organizational change—miscellaneous

Table 13.1. Action Plan for Eight Lines of Action

Line of Action	2005–2006	2006–2007	Observable Actions	Timetable
I. Build culture	Homeroom themes	Continue developing	Develop questionnaire for students, teachers' responses	September 2005
	Recognition program		For subcommittee of task force; develop questionnaire for students and faculty	September 2005
	Gregorc in-service	Gregorc for new faculty	Questionnaire re use; discussion at in-service re uses personally, professionally	July 2005, October 2005, February 2006
	Appoint students to task force; publicize	Continue student participation; continue publicity	Informal questionnaire re student impact on task force, impact of participation on student body	October 2005, Feburary 2006, May 2006
	Focus groups of students	Student focus groups	Analyze results by task force and student government; implement recommendations	October 2006, December 2006, March 2006, May 2006
Student/teacher relationships	Gegorc in-service		Questionnaire for students, faculty	July 2005, December 2005, March 2006
	Dr. Jones student engagement and motivation workshops		Questionnaire for teachers; student evaluations	July 2005, December 2005, May 2006
	Teachers' best practices		Questio:naire for teachers; student evaluations	December 2005, May 2006

	Activity	Action	Evaluation	Timeline
	Ruby Payne workshop		Teachers evaluation instrument	July 2005, December 2005, May 2006 November 2005, May 2006
	Recognition program	Continue	Teachers evaluate effectiveness	December 2005, May 2005, August 2006, December 2006, May 2007
	Dev. professional learning communities	Continue	Anecdotal evidence of teachers supporting each other; questionnaire, suggestions	December 2005, May 2006, December 2006, May 2007
Teaching techniques	Dr. Jones active learning, motivation engagement	Continue	Teachers evaluate workshops	December 2005, May 2006, December 2006, May 2007
2. Establish Ninth Grade SLC	Self videotaping analysis Ninth grade SLC begun	Expand teaming	Questionnaire for faculty, students	December 2005, May 2006, December 2006, May 2007
3. SLC teams, teaching approaches	Gregorc in-service, teaming building, trust exercises, conflict management	Continue developing with workshops as needed	Questionnaire for faculty, students	July 2005, December 2005, May 2006, December 2006, May 2007
	Trust-building exercise		Questionnaire for faculty	December 2005
	Conflict management inservice	Rerun if necessary	Questionnaire for faculty	December 2005, May 2006, December 2006, May 2007
	Develop professional learning communities	Continue developing	Questionnaire for faculty	December 2005, May 2006, December 2006, May 2007
	Mentor new teachers	Continue	Questionnaire for faculty	December 2005, May 2006, August 2006, December 2006, May 2007

(continued)

Table 13.1. *(Continued)*

Line of Action	2005–2006	2006–2007	Observable Actions	Timetable
4. Curriculum development	Development curriculum planning structure involving faculty, students, and community	Continue	Number of proposals generated and their quality	September 2005, December 2005, May 2006, August 2006, December 2006, May 2007
5. Parent community relationships				
6. Student teacher relationships, recognition committee	Form recognition committee for staff			
7. Form SLC administration teams	Form six SLC administration teams of assistant principals, guidance, clerk		In-service such as trust building, conflict management, team building	
8. Implement grant, apply for new grant	Finish ordering materials; new grant approved			

We also had heard of a National Small Schools Conference, and after some discussion, agreed to suggest that the school become one that people could visit. The Planning Committee members were a bit apprehensive about exposing themselves to outside eyes so early, to which the director of the grant for the five schools responded that the school was leagues ahead of the other four high schools, which weren't even planning yet. I mentioned that I had thought that we might focus on accomplishing two or maybe three of the eight Lines of Action, and here we were plowing into and successfully planning and implementing all eight.

For example, the ninth-grade SLC was named Renaissance, and went into operation first thing in the fall. As evidence of the significant change in the culture of the school, the Assistant Principal reported on the considerable increase in attendance (about 65 percent) and a great decrease in referrals to the office (about 55 percent).

Each of the other SLCs began working on developing their own singular theme. The grant was implemented and a new grant was applied for and awarded. The Summer Institute was huge, consisting of sixty-three different projects, which the music teacher handled with precision, expertise, and without notes. Many of these were in-service training projects, which were attended by large numbers of faculty. They included a session using the Gregorc Personality Style Delineator (1982) to help faculty and administration understand themselves, each other, and their students.

Another session was held in which Ruby Payne's (1996) insights about socioeconomic stratification were discussed and applied at considerable length by one of her certified trainees in the community. Administrative teams for each of the SLCs also spent time on in-service. Student leadership opportunities were increased.

The visitation from the Small Schools Conference turned out to be an outstanding success, with students, faculty, and staff heavily involved, and surprised at the approval and interest expressed by visitors. The school grade (Florida uses the FCAT) to grade schools moved from a low D to a high C, missing a B grade by a couple of points.

SUMMARY

We laid out the process of analyzing an organization (in this case, a school) using the Analysis of the Dynamics of Individualized Organizational Change as a strategy to reform and to decentralize a large inner city high school. The process worked quite well, although such a process takes more than a semester, obviously, to change long held norms, beliefs, and practices. Still, the school was on its way.

Key elements of the change strategy included asking people regarding their Concerns and Issues, Summarizing them (I skipped this with the Planning Task Force in view of the impatience of faculty), digging away at Underlying Themes, developing potential Lines of Action, looking for their underlying theoretical Rationales, and then settling on Lines of Action (see table B.1) to implement. Next was to develop a timetable as part of the plan. In this case, the school laid out eight Lines of Action and proceeded to go after them full blast.

The school improved considerably in this process of implementing the eight lines of action, which started with decentralizing into small learning communities, with the culture of cooperation and focus on learning considerably enhanced. SLC teams began to form, new curriculum began to emerge, community–school relationships became a major focus, a Recognition Committee began to function by recognizing anyone who did something significant, three-person SLC leadership teams began to function to head up each SLC, and the grant was implemented, with a new one developed, applied for, and won.

IMPORTANT TERMS

Indigenous leader—a natural leader who emerges when the situation calls for someone to take the lead in solving a situation, or an issue or concern

Reference group—a group that is highly respected, whom people refer to for authoritative perceptions and information

Social system—any two or more people having a meaningful relationship (such as a family or clique)

V

WHAT DID WE DO? WHY DID IT WORK? HOW CAN I DO IT? BY BUILDING AN INFRASTRUCTURE AND CULTURE TO MAKE IT WORK—ABSOLUTELY CRUCIAL

Change does not happen from the top down. It happens from the bottom up . . . (People) arguing, agitating, mobilizing, and ultimately forcing elected officials to be accountable. . . . That's how we're going to bring about change.

—Barack Obama, January 21, 2008

14

Summing Up Very Briefly: Size *Really* Matters—Decentralization Works—Seawalls Revisited

Four Infrastructures to Keep Renewal Process Surging

> He who rejects change is the architect of decay. The only human institution which rejects progress is the cemetery.
>
> —British Prime Minister Harold Wilson, January 23, 1967

THE ORGANIZATION OF THIS EXCEEDINGLY BRIEF CHAPTER

This chapter first briefly summarizes this book in six sentences. Next, we refer to the four structures and processes described in earlier chapters, which we've used successfully to defeat the forces of entropy, namely:

- A Curriculum-Steering Task Force,
- SLCs,
- PLCs,
- And last, Replanning Task Forces.

That's it.

SUMMING UP THE ORGANIZATION
OF THIS BOOK (IN SIX SENTENCES)

Time to sum up (but very, very briefly):

Section I compares and contrasts large and small schools and the assumptions favoring each. (Guess which came out with greater advantages?)

Section II lays out the dynamics and the guts of organizations, and discusses how to work effectively within and outside of them (necessary if you want to survive, let alone be effective). These were:

- Roles and role expectations
- Norms and culture
- Social systems
- Metaphors and images
- Pulls from the five parts of the organization
- The virtually inevitable organizational cycles—the forces of entropy crippling schools
- Power, authority, and influence

Section III cites other strategies (namely, the top-down model) and then lays out the major strategy used here (the Lewinian-based, bottom-up Analysis of the Dynamics of Individualized Organizational Change).

Section IV presents three case studies of large schools: a middle, an elementary, and a high school, where we used the change strategy to decentralize them—and were quite successful producing schools that improved spectacularly.

Section V refers to processes and structures described and analyzed in earlier chapters to beat the evil effects of organizational entropy (where organizations [read schools], run out of gas and become bureaucracies—whose main goal is survival).

SUMMARIZING THE FOUR STRATEGIES
TO DEFEAT THE EVIL FORCES OF ENTROPY

While this sounds a bit like a reprise of a recent movie featuring Batman (and his sidekick Robin, who live only to defeat those evil forces), we'll merely summarize four strategies that have been presented previously, so this is a very short chapter. We'll also refer to their accompanying structures to beat off the almost inevitable forces of organizational decay, called *entropy*. (Just to refresh our minds, entropy is a term first used in the physical world that describes and analyzes the inevitable decay of every physical system [computers, water pumps, walls, mountains]).

Most uncomfortably, it applies to all organizations. All organizations, including schools, decay and run out of gas, *unless you know how to counter this process by replanning.*

Reflective Question

Do all organizations have phases in their careers which lead to their decay?

You bet!
Just look at any organization over time. It changes—and, usually, for the worse. (See chapter 6 on the three phases organizations careen through in their careers, namely Person-, Plan-, and Position-orientation.) An example? How about our formerly fabled auto manufacturers? Enron? The dot coms? GM?

The Four Strategies—and Their Structures

- A Curriculum-Steering Task Force that *generates controlled change* (see chapter 4)
- SLCs, which decentralize schools (see chapters 10, 11, 12, and 13)
- PLCs (see chapter 12)
- A Replanning Task Force to overcome the inevitable forces of entropy every three years (see chapter 6)

A Curriculum-Steering Task Force or Committee to Generate Change as a Routine

Lucky you! We've already discussed this fully—how it works, along with the structure to pull it off in chapter 4, in the section on "Schools Involved in Change." It's a system designed to *produce bottom-up controlled change,* a process in which the Teachers' Associations/Unions participated fully, and which decades later is still generating change in one school system where I facilitated establishing it, which I've followed.

SLCs

The entire Section IV of three case studies in chapters 10, 11, 12, and 13 illustrates the strategies and processes involved in reforming large schools into SLCs, or houses, or halls. The case is made about the positive effects, supporting the analysis and assertions made in chapters 1 and 2, which compare and contrast large and small schools.

PLCs

The facilitative role of PLCs is presented in chapters 11, 12, and 13 (more in 12), since PLCs take time to develop. As normal issues, forces, and concerns were dealt with, people could begin thinking about more than daily survival as the structural and process changes became effective. When teacher and later Assistant Principal Lynne Menard first read and edited chapter 11, her caption regarding what teachers were going through was, "Help me, I'm drowning!"

By the time the positive effects of decentralizing began to take place, teachers began developing PLCs. They were focusing not only on improving their skills and processes, but particularly also on helping new teachers not merely to survive, but to grow and to become professional. They realized that they must make sure that the new folks wanted to stay in education, rather than be wiped out from the daily frustrations and an inability to develop personal and professional satisfactions that come from a sense of mastering teaching.

The PLCs set up processes to help teachers overcome as they focused on dealing with bottom-up issues and concerns raised. Chapter 12 indicates that the school established half day in-service sessions for the new teachers, and made sure each had a mentor. In the high school described in chapter 13, the Subplanning Council of the principal, assistant principal, the music teacher and his sidekick, and I began to take on a PLC function toward the end of year (which we all recognized after a while), particularly in planning and structuring out the summer in-service program.

Replanning Task Forces (Remember, Every Three Years—
or You Will Lose Your Plan)

The chapter that focuses on replanning is chapter 12 (replanning is also mentioned in chapter 6, which deals with the need for and the success of the replanning effort three years later to foil the fearsome forces of entropy. Brown's dissertation (2006) investigated and analyzed the success of the effort to continue the constructivist structure and teaching processes of Southwood Elementary School. His conclusion? Replanning was essential to continue the constructivist teaching and organization of the school.

And, it was done.

SUMMARY

There we have it: a brief overview of the major ideas of the book.

Appendix A

School Grade   **This school was given a grade of "A" by the Florida Department of Education in 2004. In 2003 this school received an "A."**

Math

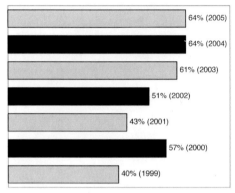

The state average for math was 63% in 2005

Reading

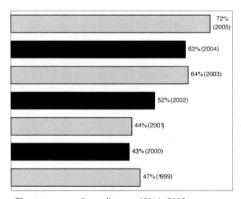

The state average for reading was 68% in 2005

Writing

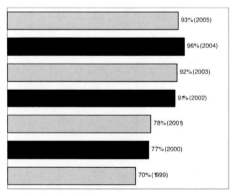

The state average for writing was 90% in 2005

Bibliography

Abramson, P. "How School Size Affects Academic Achievement." *School Planning and Management* 39, no. 5 (May 2000): 86.

Barker, R. G., and P. V. Gump. 1964. *Big school, small school.* Stanford, CA: Stanford University Press.

Barnard, C. I. *Functions of the Executive.* Cambridge, MA: Harvard University Press, 1938.

Bausch, K. C. *The Emerging Consensus in Social Systems Theory.* New York: Kluwer Academic/Plenum, 2001.

Beckhard, R. *Organization Development: Strategies and Models.* Reading, MA: Addison-Wesley, 1969.

Benjamin, W. F. "From the Curriculum Editor: The Test-Driven Curriculum." *Florida ASCD Journal* 5 (Spring 1989): 2–5.

Bickel, R., and C. B. Howley. "The Influence of Scale." *American School Board Journal* 189, no. 3 (March 2002): 28–30.

Bierstedt, R. W. "Analysis of Social Power." *American Sociological Review* 15 (1950): 730–738.

Bogardus, E. S. "Social Distance in the City." *Proceedings and Publications of the American Sociological Society* 20 (1926): 40–46.

Bolman, L. G., and T. E. Deal. *Reframing Organizations: Artistry, Choice, and Leadership.* San Francisco: Jossey-Bass, 1991.

Brantlinger, E. "Social Class in School: Students' Perspectives." *Research Bulletin of Phi Delta Kappa* 14 (March 1995): 1–4.

Brown, J. C. "A Case Study of a School Implementing a Constructivist Philosophy." PhD diss., University of South Florida, *Dissertation Abstracts International*, 2006.

Burley, W. W., and A. S. Shapiro. "Beliefs, Symbols, and Realities: A Case Study of a School in Transition." In *Changing American Education: Recapturing the Past or Inventing the Future?* Edited by K. M. Borman and N. P. Greenman, 325–350. Albany, NY: State University of New York Press, 1994.

Bryk, A. S. "Measuring Achievement Gains in the Chicago Public Schools." In A. Bryk, Y. M. Thum, J. Q. Easton, and S. Luppescu, "Assessing School Academic Productivity: The Case of Chicago School Reform." *Social Psychology of Education* 2, no. 1 (March 1997): 103–142.

Bryk, A. S., Deabster, P. E., Easton, J. Q., Luppescu, S. and Y. M. Thum. *Measuring Achievement Gains in the Chicago Public Schools.* Newbury Park, CA: Sage: Education and Urban Society 26(3) (1994): 3.

Bryk, A. S., and B. Schneider. *Trust in Schools: A Core Resource for Improvement.* New York: Russell Sage Foundation, 2002.

Clauset, K. H. *Schoolwide Action Research for Professional Learning Communities: Improving Student Learning through the Whole-Faculty Study Groups Approach.* Thousand Oaks, CA: Corwin, 2008.

Conant, J. B. *The American High School Today.* New York: McGraw-Hill, 1959.

Cotton, K. *Affective and Social Benefits of Small-Scale Schooling.* Charleston, WV: Clearinghouse for Rural and Small Schools, Appalachia Educational Laboratory, 1996.

———. *New Small Learning Communities: Findings from Recent Literature.* Portland, OR: Northwest Regional Educational Laboratory, 2001.

Deming, W. E. *Quality, Productivity, and Competitive Position.* Cambridge, MA: Massachusetts Institute of Technology, Center for Advanced Engineering Study, 1982.

Dewey, J. *Experience and Education.* New York: Macmillan, 1938.

Dunlap, D. M., and P. Goldman. "Rethinking Power in Schools." *Educational Administrative Quarterly* 27, no. 1 (1991): 5–29.

Eckman, J. M., and C. B. Howley, eds. *Sustainable Small Schools: A Handbook for Rural Communities.* Charleston, WV: ERIC Clearinghouse on Rural and Small Schools. Appalachia Educational Laboratory, 1997.

English, F. W. "Caveat Emptor: A Deconstructive Reading of the Stealth Metaphysics of Stephen R. Covey." *Educational Leadership Review* 3, no. 3 (2002): 13–22.

Follett, M. P. *Creative Experience.* New York: Peter Smith, 1924.

Fowler, W. J., Jr., and H. J. Walberg. "School Size, Characteristics, and Outcomes." *Educational Evaluation and Policy Analysis* 13, no. 2 (1991): 189–202.

French J. P. R., Jr., and B. H. Raven. "The Basis of Social Power." In *Studies in Social Power,* edited by D. Cartwright, 150–167. Ann Arbor, MI: Institute for Social Research, 1959.

French, T. *South of Heaven: Welcome to High School at the End of the Twentieth Century.* New York: Doubleday, 1993.

Garbarino, J. "The Human Ecology of School Crime: A Case for Small Schools. In *School Crime and Disruption: Prevention Models,* edited by E. Wenk and N. Harlow. Washington, DC: U.S. Department of Education, National Institute of Education, 1978.

Getzels, J. W., and E. G. Guba. "Social Behavior and Administrative Process." *School Review* 65 (Winter 1957): 429. Chicago: University of Chicago Press.

Getzels, J. W., and H. A. Thelen. "The Classroom Group as a Social System." In *The Dynamics of Instructional Groups: Sociopsychological Aspects of Teaching and Learning*, edited by N. B. Henry. N.S.S.E. Yearbook 59, no. 2 (1960): 80. Chicago: National Society for the Study of Education.

Gleick, J. *Chaos: Making a New Science*. New York: Penguin, 1987.

Godfredson, D. C. *School Size and School Disorder*. Baltimore, MD: Johns Hopkins University, Center for Social Organization of Schools (ERIC Document Retrieval Service No. ED261456), 1985.

Gregorc, A. F. *Gregorc Style Delineator*. Columbia, CT: Gregorc Associates, Inc., 1982.

Gregory, T. B., and G. R. Smith. *High Schools as Communities: The Small School Reconsidered*. Bloomington, IN: Phi Delta Kappa Foundation, 1987.

Gross, N., W. S. Mason, and A. W. McEachern. *Explorations in Role Analysis: Studies of the School Superintendency Role*. New York: Wiley, 1966.

Halpin, A. *Administrative Theory in Action*. London: Macmillan, 1958.

Halpin, A. W., and D. B. Croft. "Organizational Climate of Schools." *Administrator's Notebook* 11, no. 7 (March 1963): 1–4.

Hanvey, R. *The Idea of Liberty in American Culture*. Chicago, IL: Anthropology Curriculum Study Project, American Anthropology Association, 1963.

Hare, D. and J. Heap (2001). *Effective Teacher Recruitment and Retention Strategies in the Midwest: Who Is Making Use of Them?* Naperville, IL: North Central Regional Educational Laboratory.

Hensley, R. "Issues Present When Entering a System." In *The 1982 Annual for Facilitators, Trainers, and Consultants*, edited by J. W. Pfeiffer and L. D. Goodstein. San Diego, CA: University Associates, 1982.

Howard, E. "There May Be No Fair Play in American Rigged Schools." *Changing Schools*. Muncie, IN: Teacher's College 918, Ball State University, 1989.

Hunt, J. J., W. F. Benjamin, and A. S. Shapiro. *What Florida Teachers Say About the FCAT*. Tampa. FL: ETC, 2004.

Isaacson, L. S. 2004. Teachers' Perceptions of Constructivism as an Organizational Change Model: A Case Study. PhD diss., University of South Florida, *Dissertation Abstracts International*, 2004.

Jones, T., and T. Gilliam. *Monty Python's the Meaning of Life*. (Motion picture). Universal Pictures, 1983.

Katz, R. L. "Skills of an Effective Administrator." *Harvard Business Review* 33 (1955): 33–42.

Kohlberg, L. *The Philosophy of Moral Development: Moral Stages and Idea of Justice*. San Francisco: Harper & Row, 1981.

Komives, S. R., N. Lucas, and T. R. McMahon. *Exploring Leadership for College Students Who Want to Make a Difference*. San Francisco: Jossey-Bass, 1998.

Koren, A., and V. Logaj. *When a Teacher Becomes a Head Teacher: Research on Newly Appointed Head Teachers*. Manuscript submitted for publication, 2009.

Koren, A., and A. Shapiro. "Are Educators Lemmings? Now It's Standards—Another Behaviorist Hoax." Unpublished manuscript, 2009.

Kozol, J. *Savage Inequalities: Children in America's Schools*. New York: Crown, 1991.

Lambert, L., M. Collay, M. E. Dietz, K. Kent, and A. E. Richert. *Who Will Save Our Schools? Teachers as Constructivist Leaders*. Thousand Oaks, CA: Corwin, 1996.

Lambert, L., D. Walker, D. P. Zimmerman, J. E. Cooper, M. D. Lambert, M. E. Gardner, and P. J. Ford Slack. *The Constructivist Leader.* New York: Teachers College, 1995.

Lammers, J. "Sociology of Organizations around the Globe: Convergences and Divergences." Unpublished paper presented at the Annual Meeting of the American Sociological Association, Chicago, 1987.

Lee, V., and J. Smith. "Effects of High School Restructuring and Size on Gains in Achievement and Engagement for Early Secondary School Students." *Sociology of Education* 68, no. 4 (1995): 241–270.

———. "High School Size: Which Works Best and For Whom?" *Educational Evaluation and Policy Analysis* 19, no. 3 (1997): 205–227.

Lee, V., J. Smith, and R. Croninger. "How High School Organization Influences the Equitable Distribution of Learning in Mathematics and Science." *Sociology of Education* 70, no. 2 (April 1997): 128–150.

Leggett, S., C. W. Brubaker, A. Cohodes, and A. S. Shapiro. *Planning Flexible Learning Places.* New York: McGraw-Hill, 1977.

Leggett, S., and A. S. Shapiro. "An Analysis and Commentary on Policy and Rules #5000 as Amended August 18, 1983 by the School Board of Broward County: Subject: Adequate Educational Facilities, Designation of Schools and Attendance Areas, Elimination and Consolidation of Schools." Martha's Vineyard: Stanton Leggett and Associates, 1983. (An Analysis Undertaken for the City of Fort Lauderdale.)

Levinson, D. *The Seasons of a Man's Life.* New York: Knopf, 1978.

Lewin, K. "Group Decision and Social Change." In *Readings in Social Psychology,* Edited by T. M. Newcomb and E. L. Hartley. New York: Holt, 1952.

Lindsey, P. "The Effect of High School Size on Student Participation, Satisfaction, and Attendance." *Educational Evaluation and Policy Analysis* 4 (1982): 57–65.

Linton, R. *Tree of Culture.* New York: Random House, 1955.

Luciano, P. R. "The Systems View of Organizations: Dynamics of Organizational Change." In *1979 Annual for Facilitators, Trainers, and Consultants,"* edited by J. W. Pfeiffer and L. D. Goodstein, 140–145. San Diego, CA: University Associates, 1979.

Macy, J. "Viewpoints." *Noetic Sciences Bulletin* (Winter 1994–1995): 2.

Maslow, A. H. *Motivation and Personality.* New York: Harper & Row, 1954.

Meier, D. "Small Schools: As Though They Owned the Place." *Phi Delta Kappan* 87, no. 9: 657–662.

Mintzberg, H. *The Rise and Fall of Strategic Planning: Reconceiving Roles for Planning, Plans, and Planners.* New York: Free Press, 1994.

———. *The Structuring of Organizations.* Englewood Cliffs, NJ: Prentice-Hall, 1979.

Mish, F. C. *Webster's Ninth New Collegiate Dictionary.* Springfield, MA: Merriam-Webster, 1988.

Monk, D. "Do Larger High Schools Offer Better Curriculum?" *Journal of the New York State School Boards Association* (August 1987): 11–12.

Morgan, G. *Images of Organizations.* Thousand Oakes, CA: Sage, 1997.

Muncey, D. E., and P. J. McQuillan. "Preliminary Findings from a Five-Year Study of the Coalition of Essential Schools." *Phi Delta Kappan* (February 1993): 486–489.

Nathan, J., and K. Febey. *Smaller, Safer, Saner Successful Schools.* Washington, DC: Center for Educational Facilities, Center for School Change, Humphrey Institute of the University of Minnesota, Minneapolis, MN, 2001.

Oakes, J. *Keeping Track: How Schools Structure Inequality.* New Haven, CT: Yale University Press, 1985.

Oldroyd, D. "Educational Leadership for Results or for Learning? Contrasting Directions in Times of Transition." *Managing Global Transitions: International Research Journal* 1 (Spring 2003): 49–67.

Owens, R. *Organizational Behavior in Education.* 6th ed. Boston: Allyn & Bacon, 1988.

Oxley, D. "Smaller is Better." *American Educator* 13, no. 1 (1989): 28–31, 42–51.

———. "Theory and Practice of School Communities." *Educational Administration Quarterly* 33 (1997a): 624–643.

———. "Theory and practice of school communities." *Educational Administration Quarterly* 33, (1997b): 624–643.

Parsons, T., and E. A. Shils, eds. *Toward a General Theory of Action: Theoretical Foundations for the Social Sciences.* Cambridge, MA: Harvard University Press, 1951.

Pascale, R. T. *Managing on the Edge.* New York: Simon & Schuster, 1990.

Payne, R. *A Framework for Understanding Poverty.* Highlands, TX: Aha! Process, Inc., 1996.

Pittman, R., and P. Haughwout. "Influence of High School Size on Dropout Rate. *Educational Evaluation and Policy Analysis* 9 (1987): 337–343.

Raywid, M. *Current Literature on Small Schools.* Charleston, WV: Clearinghouse on Rural Education and Small Schools, Appalachia Educational Laboratory, 1999.

———. *Taking Stock: The Movement to Create Mini-Schools, Schools within Schools, and Separate Small Schools.* New York: Columbia University, Teachers College, ERIC Clearinghouse on Urban Education, 1996.

Reed, M., and M. Hughes. *Rethinking Organization: New Directions in Organization Theory and Analysis.* Thousand Oaks, CA: Sage, 1992.

Sarason, S. *Revisiting "The Culture of the School and the Problem of Change."* New York: Teachers College, Columbia University Press, 1996.

Shapiro, A. "Designing Our Structures to Do Our Heavy Lifting: What a Curriculum Structure Can Do to Make Our Lives *A Lot* Easier." In *Case Studies in Constructivist Leadership and Teaching,* 287–304. Lanham, MD: Scarecrow, 2003.

———. "The Dynamics of Individualized Change: Organizational Mapping, a Construct to Diagnose, Plan, and Implement Organizational Change." In *Leadership and Diversity in Education: Second Yearbook,* edited by J. L. Burdin, 86–94. National Council of Professors of Educational Administration (NCPEA). Lancaster, PA: Technomic, 1994.

———. *Leadership for Constructivist Schools.* Lanham, MD: Scarecrow, 2000.

———. *The Effective Constructivist Leader: A Guide to the Successful Approaches.* Lanham, MD: Rowman & Littlefield, 2008.

Shapiro, A., W. F. Benjamin, and J. J. Hunt. *Curriculum and Schooling: A Practitioner's Guide.* Palm Springs, CA: ETC, 1995.

Shapiro, A., and A. S. Thompson. "Why Band-Aids Don't Work: Analyzing and Evaluating No Child Left Behind (NCLB) in Light of Constructivist Philosophy,

Theory, and Practice." *Journal of the Oxford Round Table, Forum on Public Policy* (Summer 2009).

Sheehy, G. *Passages*. New York: Bantam, 1977.

Steinhoff, C. R. *Organizational Climate in a Public School System*. U.S.O.E. Cooperative Research Program, Contract no. OE-4-225, Project no. S-083, Syracuse University, New York, 1965.

Taylor, F. W. *The Principles of Scientific Management*. New York: Harper & Row, 1911.

Thelen, H. A. "Group Dynamics in Instruction: The Principle of Least Group Size. *School Review* (March 1949): 139–148.

VanMaanen, J., and E. H. Schein. *Organizational Careers: Some New Perspectives*. London: Wiley & Sons, 1979.

Walberg, H. J., and W. J. Fowler, Jr. "Expenditure and Size Efficiencies of Public School Districts." *Educational Researcher* 16, no. 7 (1987): 5–13.

Wasley, P. H., M. Fine, M. Gladden, N. E. Holland, S. O. King, E. Mosak, and L. C. Powell. *Small Schools, Great Strides: A Study of New Small Schools in Chicago*. New York: Bank Street College of Education, 2000.

Weber, M. In *From Max Weber: Essays in Sociology*, edited by H. H. Gerth and C. W. Mills, 180–195. New York: Oxford University Press, 1946.

Weber, M. "Influence under Behavior of Others." In *Formal Organizations*. Edited by P. M. Blau and W. R. Scott, 27–32. San Francisco: Chandler Publishing, 1962.

Wehlage, G., G. Smith, and P. Lipman. "Restructuring Urban Schools: The New Futures Experience." *American Educational Research Journal* 29, no. 1 (Spring 1992): 51–93.

Wilson, L. C., T. M. Byar, A. S. Shapiro, and S. H. Schell. *Sociology of Supervision: An Approach to Comprehensive Planning in Education*. Boston: Allyn & Bacon, 1969.

About the Author

Arthur Shapiro (PhD, University of Chicago) is a theoretically based practitioner who is Professor of Education in the College of Education at the University of South Florida, Tampa, Florida.

He has been a high school, middle school, and elementary teacher, a senior high school principal, director of secondary education (twice), assistant superintendent, and superintendent of schools, all in nationally prominent districts. He has developed nongraded high schools and elementary schools, as well as schools of choice. His experience covers working in and with public and private schools in inner-city, urban, suburban, and rural settings, plus two nationally famous laboratory schools, one being John Dewey's Lab School at the University of Chicago. He has also served on two boards of education, chairing the education committee of one.

His teaching is based on modeling a constructivist philosophy and approach, for which he received the TIP award for excellence in teaching.

Dr. Shapiro's writing and consulting are empirically based on his wide experience. He is a pioneer in the small schools and small learning communities (SLC) movement, having published articles about and developed decentralized schools as a director of secondary education, assistant superintendent, and superintendent. He consults internationally and nationally in leadership, organization, and management; change strategies and developing comprehensive system-wide planning models; and analyzing, planning, and implementing change strategies that work. He consults in personality and learning styles, conflict-resolution strategies, team and trust building, establishing oneself as a leader, etc.

He was lead author of an analysis and comprehensive recommendations to improve the Republic of Macedonia's radical school reform, which decentralized their entire system into independent school districts (all 2,500 schools). He provided expertise in analyzing the radical school reform of the entire school system of the Republic of Georgia, with recommendations for improvement.

His major publications include three of the first five books on constructivist leadership, the first new theory of leadership since the late 1970s.

Dr. Shapiro served on the Working Committee for Desegregation of the Hillsborough County Schools in Florida as the only outsider, and on the Committee for Instructional Design. He has been and is chair and co-chair of numerous dissertation committees, also serving on university, college, and departmental committees.

He admires his talented wife, Sue, and two adult children, one of whom, Marc, is a PhD in Political Science and Policy Analysis, and an international consultant, and Alana Shapiro Thompson, who teaches English Literature at Tennessee State University in Nashville, Tennessee, and is working on her doctorate.

Unfortunately (and sadly), he is an unrequited, almost a compulsive, punster, much to the chagrin of his decreasing number of friends.